OPUS 28

EMILY

A HOUSE ORGAN BY A. DAVID MOORE

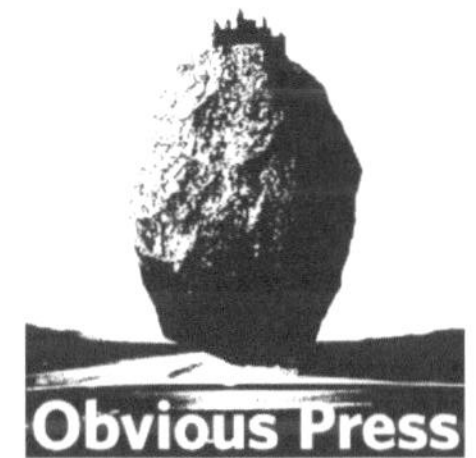

MIRIAM ZACH & MIKESCH MUECKE

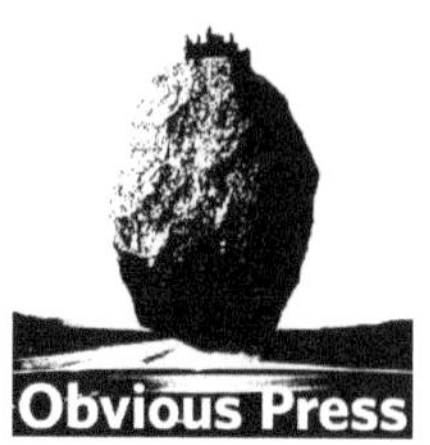

Obvious Press
918 5th Street
Ames, IA, 50010
USA
www.obviouspress.com

First published in 2006; second edition in 2008; third edition 2016
OPUS 28 - EMILY: A HOUSE ORGAN BY A. DAVID MOORE.

ISBN: 978-1-941892-20-6

Designed by polytekton and Meg Moore.

Table of Contents

Overview

Project Information:
One-manual, four-rank tracker pipe organ with separate blower and pedal

Location:
Gainesville, Florida

Designer/Builder:
A. David Moore & Co.
Pomfret, Vermont

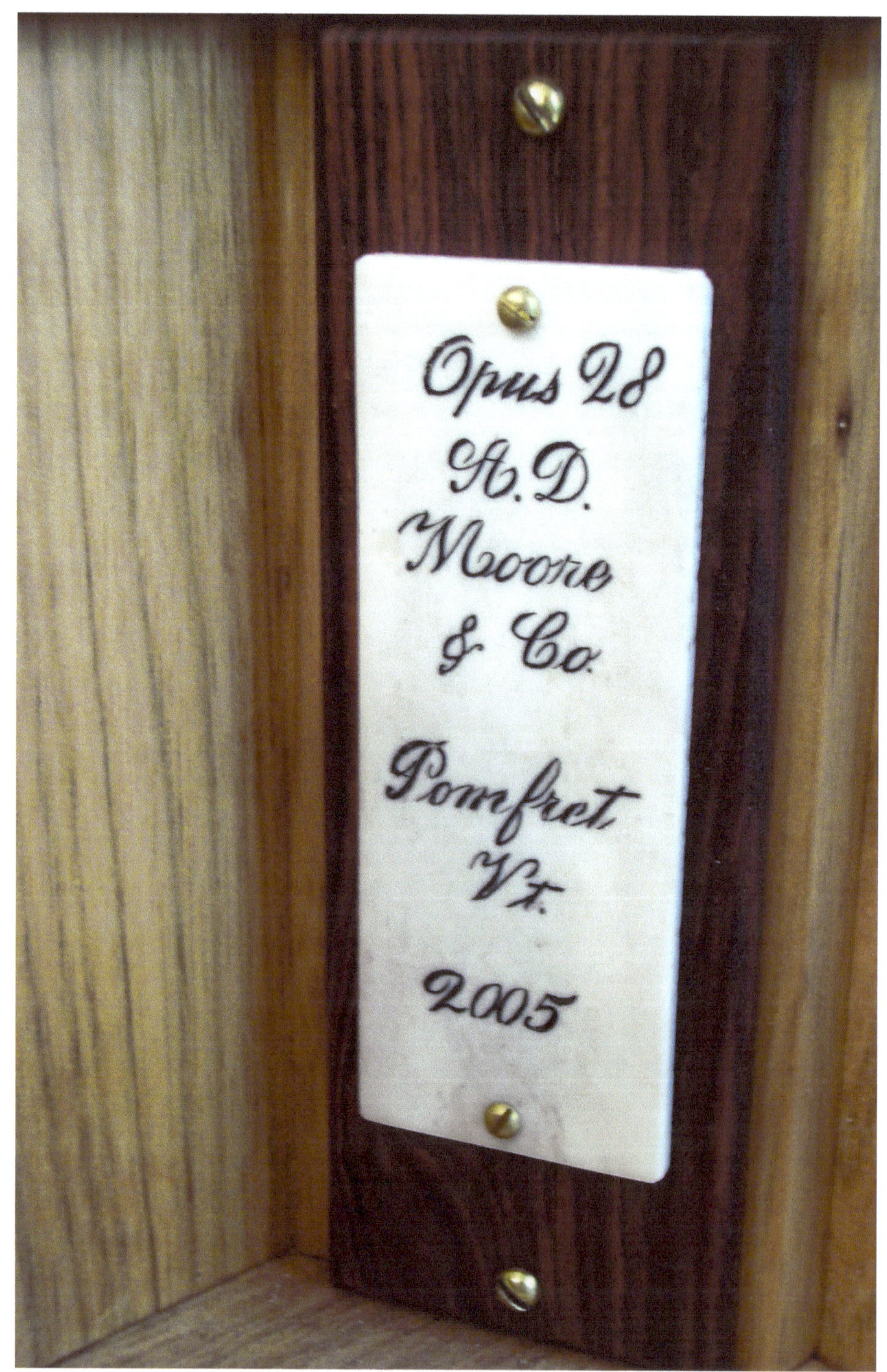

Op. 28, Emily, was designed and built by A. David Moore of Pomfret, Vermont, assisted by Thomas Bowen, John Atwood, and Thaddeus Stamps. Commissioned by Miriam Zach, Mikesch Mücke and Margaret Zach for the International Women Composers Library in August 2004, it was installed in July 2005 in Gainesville, Florida.

The clarity and subtle beauty of the sound of the pipes of Op. 28, its lovely solid wood-carved casework with bench, and direct precise key action all contribute to the aesthetic pleasure and salubrious experience of the organist and listeners alike in an innovative design.

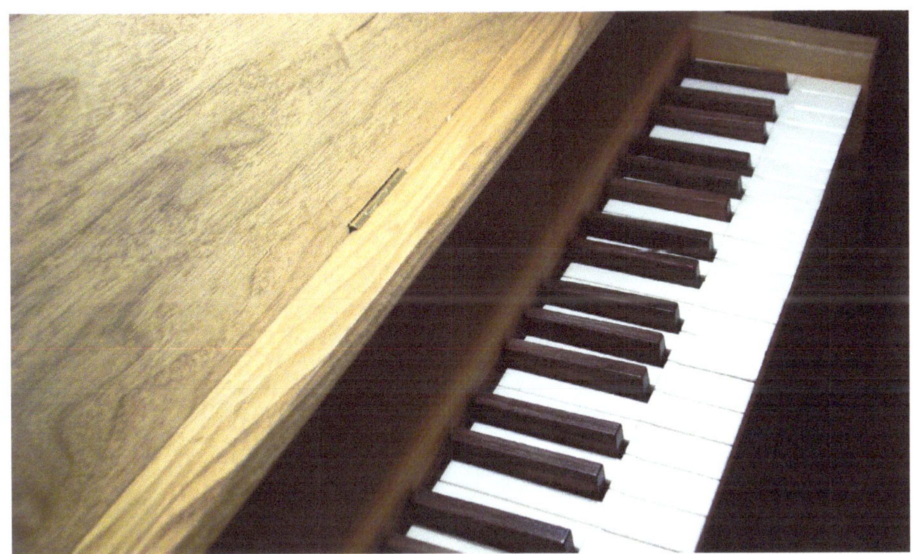

Op. 28 is made completely of natural solid wood (no plywood) with beautiful joinery and creative care in details. Black Cherry, Butternut, and Ash came from A. David Moore's forest in Vermont. He and his colleagues cut trees and ran them through the sawmill on his property. The intricate case carving and bench are Black Cherry. The case and front pipes are Butternut. Pedal pipes are Ash. A few wooden parts come from other regions. Close-Grain Oak in pipe caps comes from Germany. Toeboards are Western Red Cedar. Sharps and stop knobs are made of Rosewood. Bench height adjustment blocks are Black Cherry. There are no metal pipes. The only metal parts are copper tubing connecting the pedal windchest and pedal pipes, lead pedal tuners, and pedal-to-valve connection rods. A mixture of 75% linseed oil +25% mineral spirits cares for the wood.

The action is direct, i.e. the keyboard is suspended at the tail of the keys which push stickers down to open the valves in the chest. Pedals are square with a roller board and pull directly. There is no coupler, i.e. when the organ is on, pedals are on, unless the pedal windway is disconnected from the blower. An auxillary pedal cover made of Cherry wood may be placed over the pedal pipes.

Details

The intricate carving on the case, executed in Black Cherry, is by David Laro. The origin of the carving can be traced back to the *Lippische Rose* symbol of Lemgo, Germany, and the spiral, a symbol of the International Women Composers Library. The casework consists of Stickley-style side and back panels, and a case front with speaking façade pipes and organic ornament. Case wood is Butternut with Cherry trim. The lid folds up to transform itself into the music rack. The main case is freestanding and mobile with four removable screw-in carrying handles.

The keyboard (56 notes, CC-g3) has Rosewood sharps and Bone keys; it is transposable with lift-slide-push/pull mechanism, and when

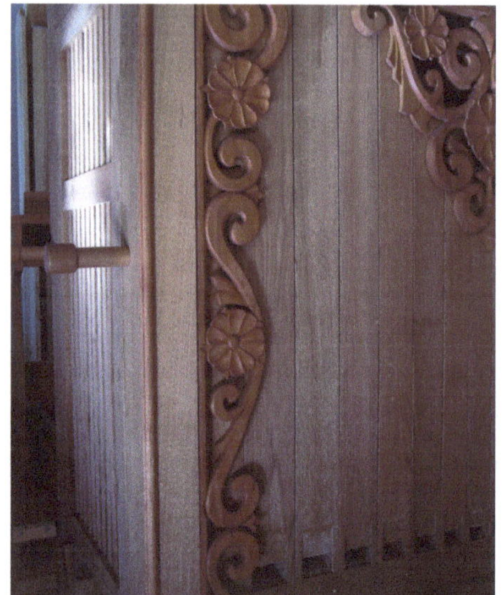

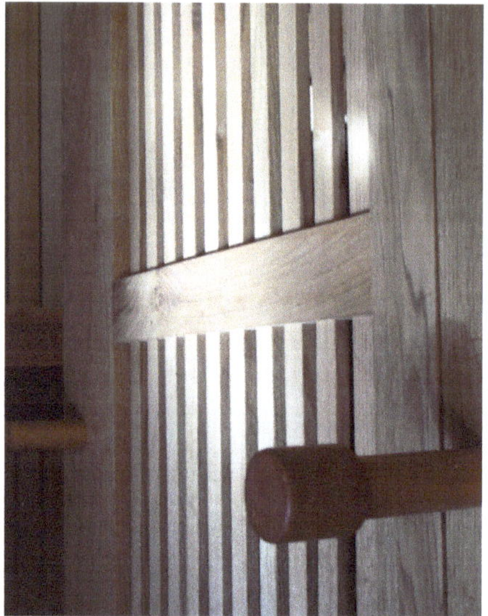

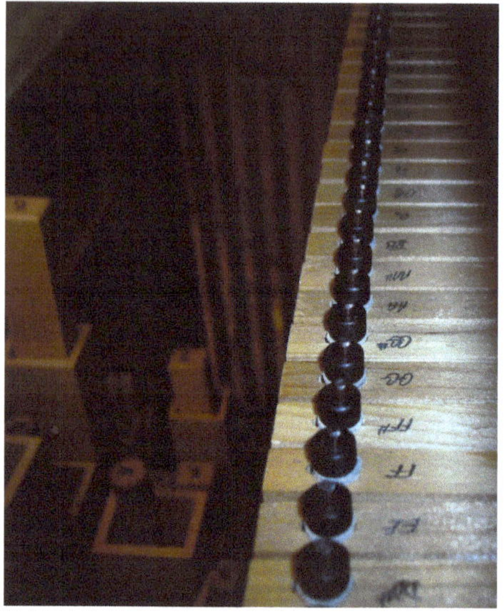

the main case is moved, the keyboard slides into case. The straight pedalboard (30 notes, CC - f1) is of Cherry and Maple. Key action is mechanical, suspended, and direct. The carved bench and high chair (when organ is moved) is of Black Cherry. Stop labels are hand engraved and the stop knobs are of Rosewood.

The all-wooden pipes represent the voices of A. David Moore's trees in Pomfret, Vermont.

There are four sets of pipes (Manual 8'4'2' and Pedal) made of Ash, Butternut, Maple, and Pine. The 8' Stopped Diapason - display front - is of Butternut, the 4' Flute - bottom octave - is a stopped bass, the middle two octaves are wooden chimney flutes, and the top octave and half are wooden stop pipes. The 2' Fifteenth is an open wood. The Pedal - 8' open - is on all the time (no coupler) and made of Ash.

The blower is located in a separate solid Butternut wooden box (which includes a carved wooden holder for a 6'-long 120 Volt cable and plug) with removable screw-in carrying handles; the wind pressure is 2.3 inches, provided by a very quiet blower motor made by August Laukhuff in Germany. The windchest is standard with stickers and pallet.

Innovation

How is Op. 28 an innovative design in pipe organs?

1. It is unusual to be able to stand an organ on its end to easily reach the pallet box, which contains springs that hold the keys up.

2. Op. 28 has a transposable keyboard (a'=440 HZ) that can be moved down 1/2 step for playing early music. It uses the same CC for CC so if the keyboard is transposed, it is necessary to retune CC. Pipes are tuned in the Bach-Kellner temperament, which is good for playing in many keys. A. David Moore used the German-made Vogel-Scheer electronic tuner CTS-32L with stroboscopic display to tune the organ after installation.

3. Several design considerations contribute to easy portability

of the case containing the keyboard and 8', 4', and 2' pipes, which are disconnected from the pedals. The case is freestanding with handles on each side that are easily unscrewed. The keyboard slides into the box. The top cover is hinged and folds up to serve a dual function as the music rack. The case weighs approximately 170 pounds. The keyboard is high so the player may sit on a high chair or stand up to play when the case is removed from the pedals. The blower is in a separate solid Butternut wooden box with easily removable handles. The blower box weighs approximately 50 pounds, so it, too, is easily transportable for concerts and educational outreach.

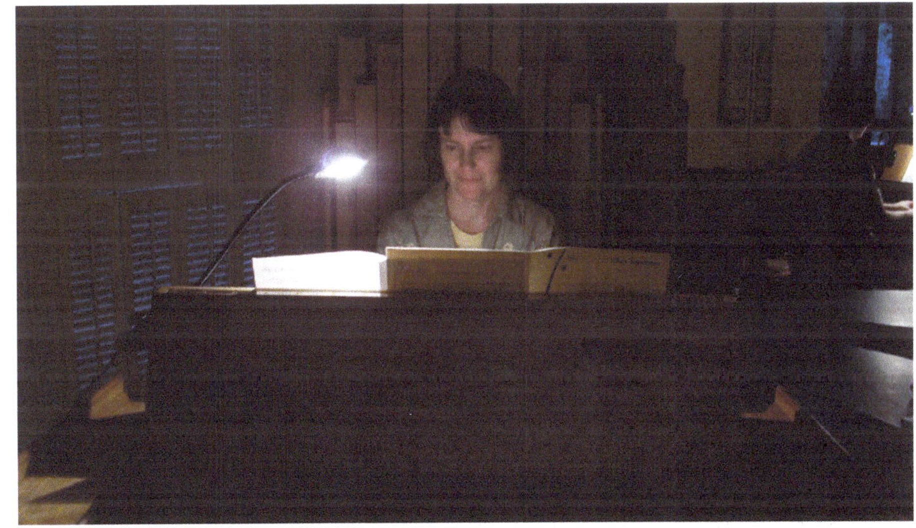

- Notes by Dr. Miriam Zach, Assistant Professor of Music in the Honors Program, University of Florida, Gainesville, and Director of the International Women Composers Library

Part of this text was also published in *The American Organist,* June 2006, page 97.

Design

David Moore provided us with an initial design for Opus 28 in the late summer of 2004. It called for an almost square shape (44 inches high by 45 inches wide) with a simple two-panel back face (where the keyboard is located) and a front face with speaking facade pipes, decorated by a central triangular ornament.

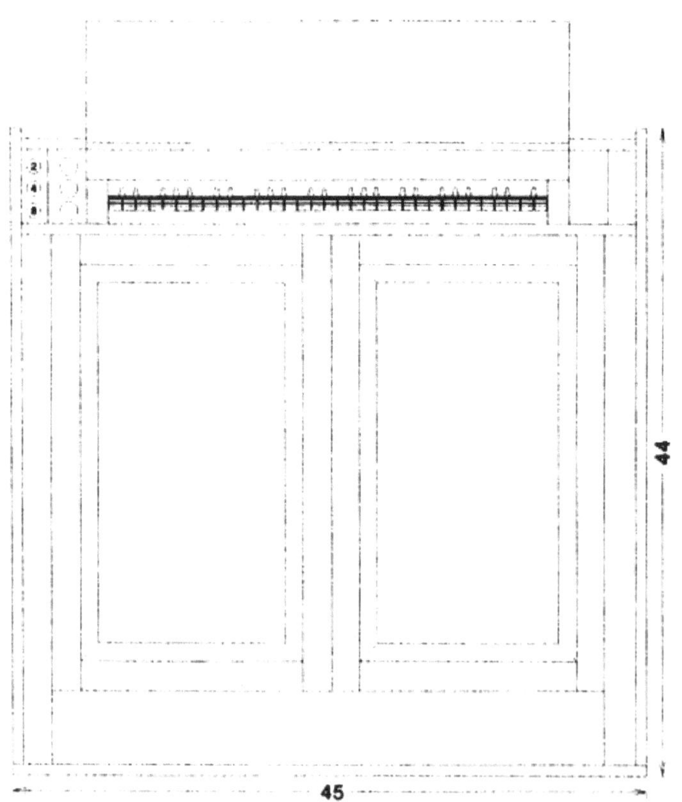

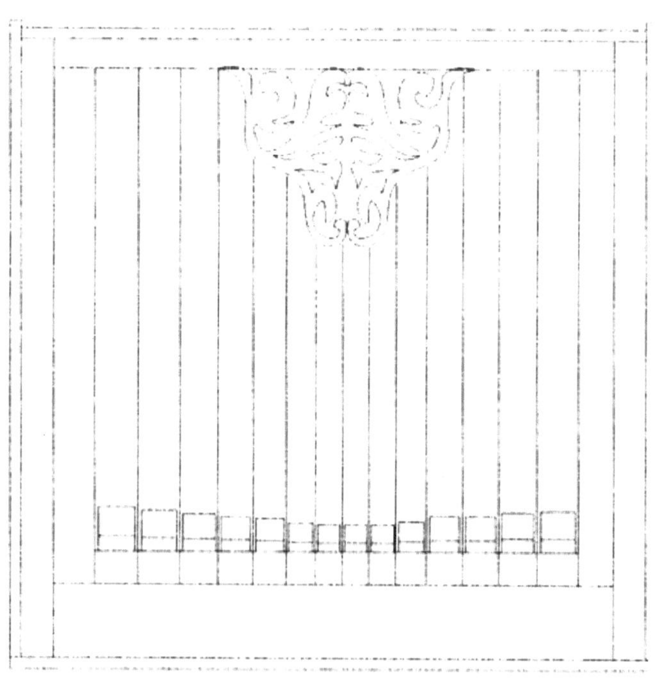

Sketches developed by David Moore for Opus 28, Emily.

For the organ ornament Mikesch offered to design two narrow vertical pieces on each side of the front facade, in addition to the central triangular ornament. Below are some floral inspirations and to the right two examples for possible designs. Miriam wanted to include the *Lippische Rose* as a design element (visible in red).

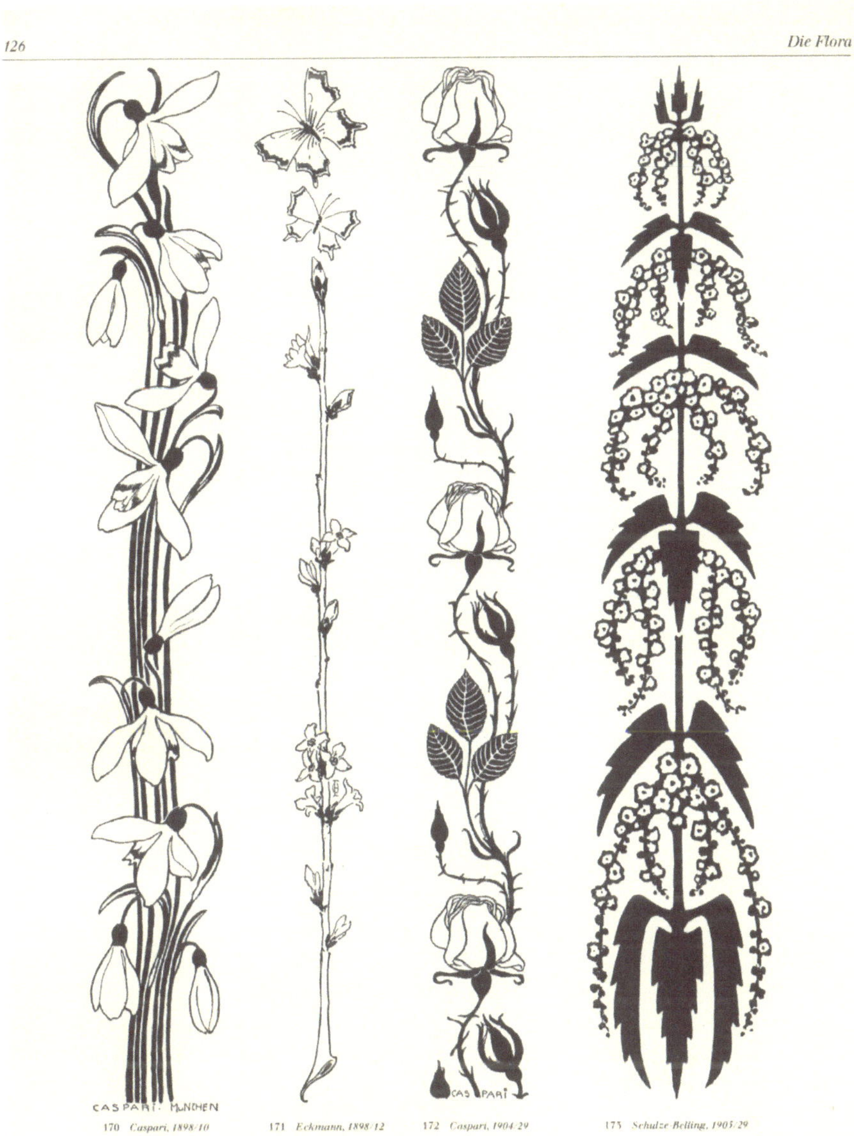

126 *Die Flora*

CASPARI · MÜNCHEN

CASPARI

170 *Caspari, 1898/10* 171 *Eckmann, 1898/12* 172 *Caspari, 1904/29* 173 *Schulze-Belling, 1905/29*

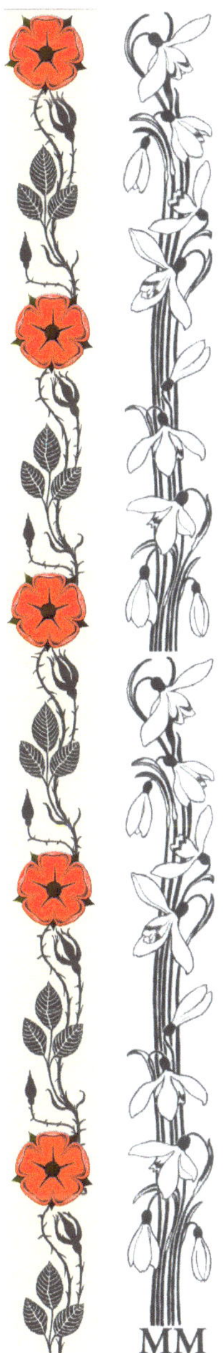

In order to be able to visualize the effect of the ornament on the facade, Mikesch created a digital model in 3D and tested the ornamentation through a series of renderings. The final design is depicted below. However, the wood carver David Laro, who would do the actual carving, had the final say in how the design would work with the carving strategy. His final design varied substantially from this version, without sacrificing any of the beauty of the carved wood.

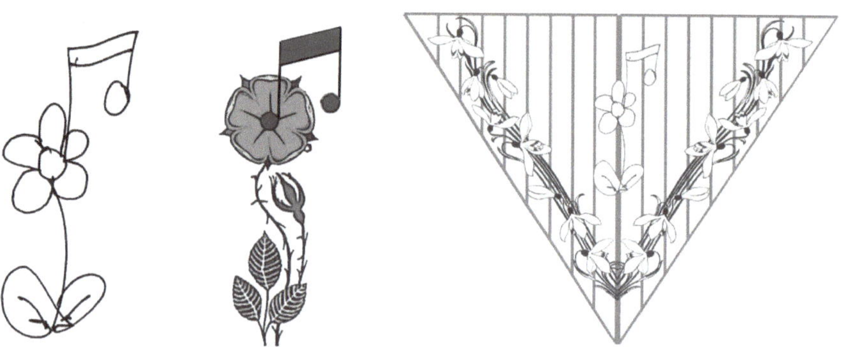

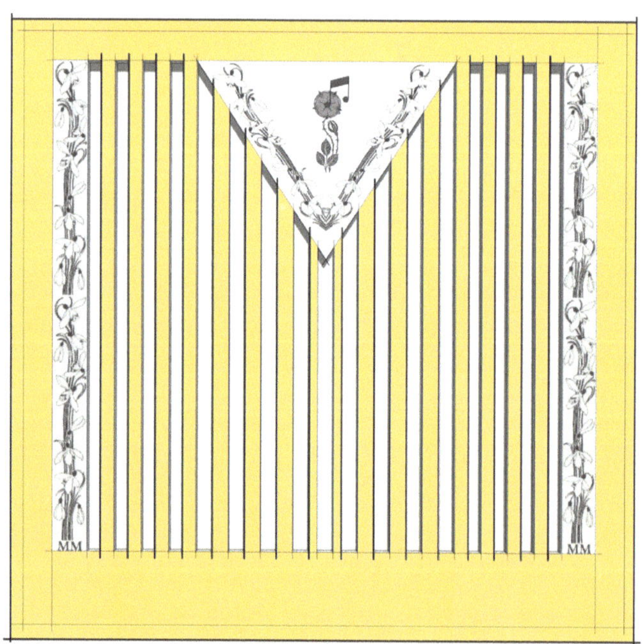

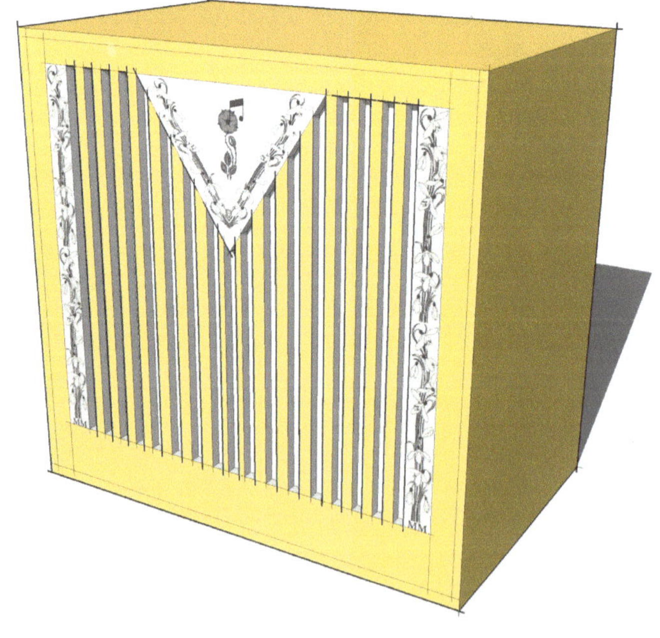

Anticipation

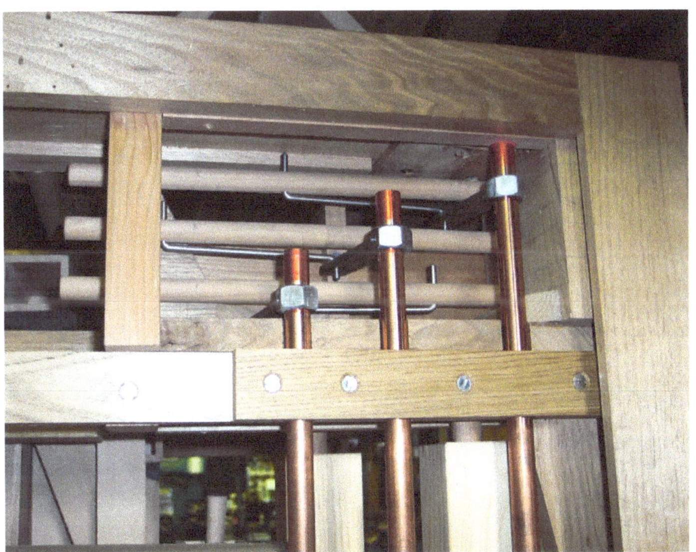

In the fall of 2004 Miriam was giving a concert in Troy, New York, and we decided to visit David Moore's workshop in Pomfret, Vermont. We arrived in the late afternoon on a bright September day and as we entered the studio we saw David play what would become Emily, silhouetted against the sun light. Until then we did not have a contract but at the end of our visit Miriam had decided to commission Opus 28 by David Moore.

While we were waiting for the organ, A. David Moore sent the following images to us via email so that we could get an idea about how far along the design had progressed in his workshop in Vermont.

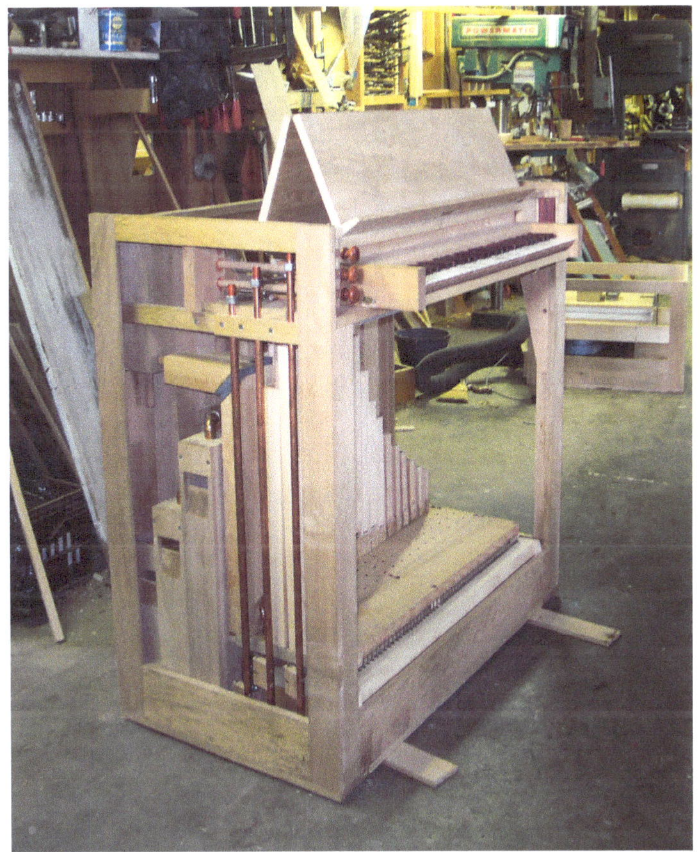

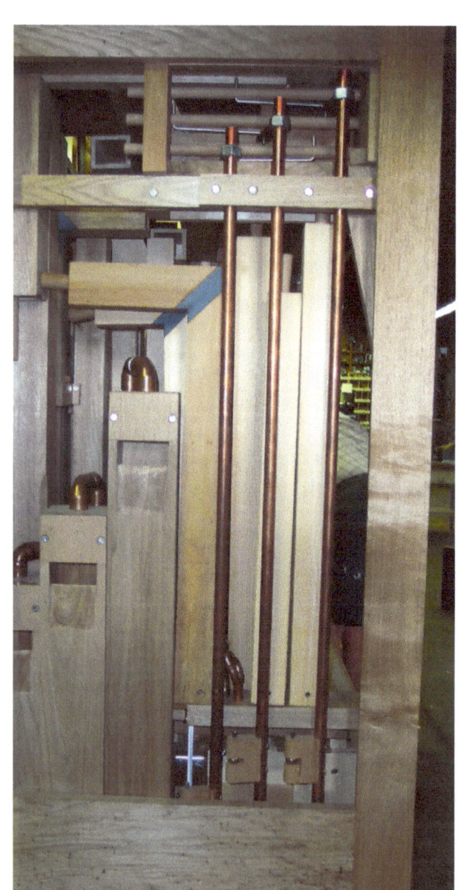

Views of Opus 28, Emily, under construction in David Moore's workshop in Pomfret, Vermont.

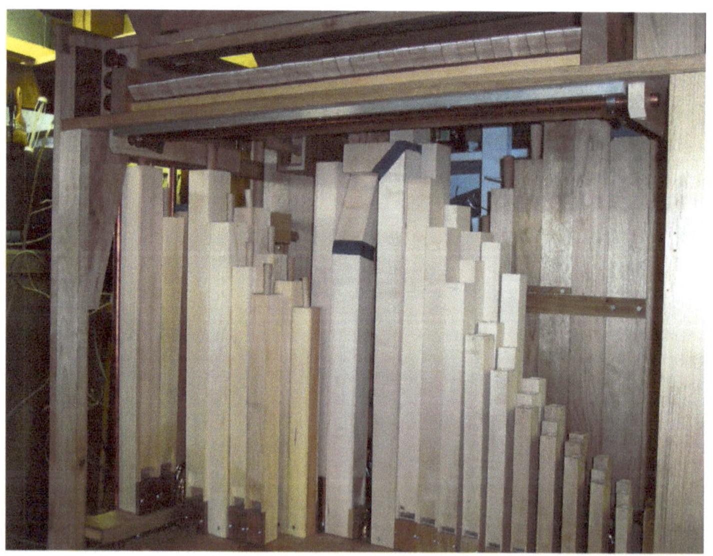

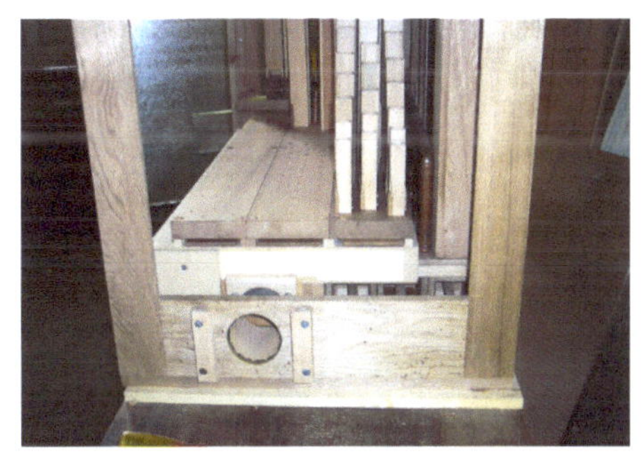

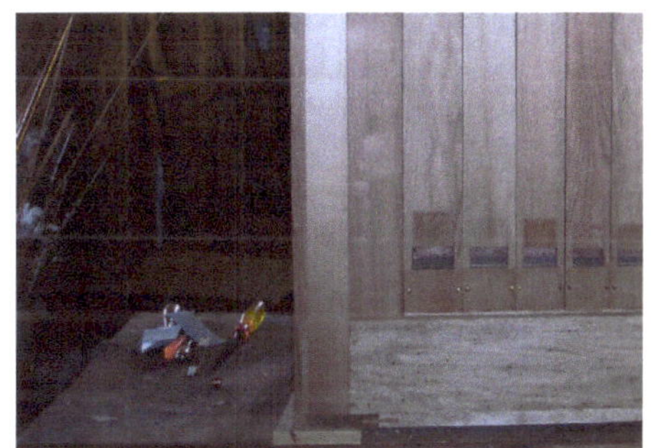

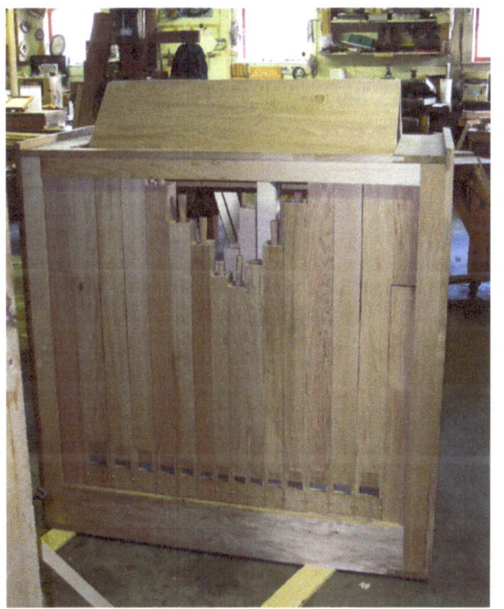

Delivery

Opus 28, Emily, arrived on the evening of July 26, 2005 in Gainesville in David Moore's blue van. Rather than unpack that night in the dark, David decided to wait until the next morning. Mikesch went out before night fall to take a first peek at the beauty that lay all dissected in the cargo hold of the van.

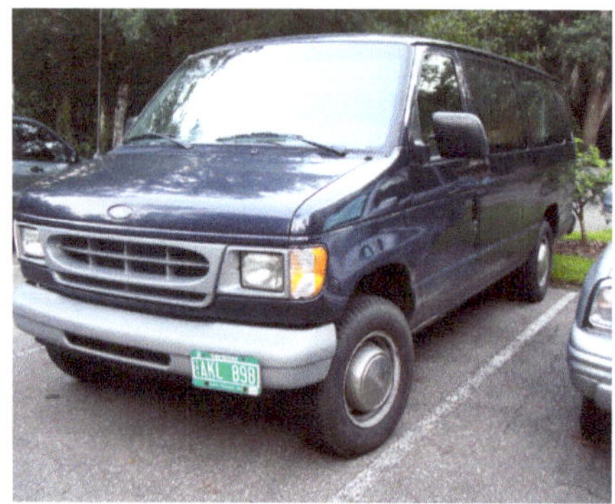

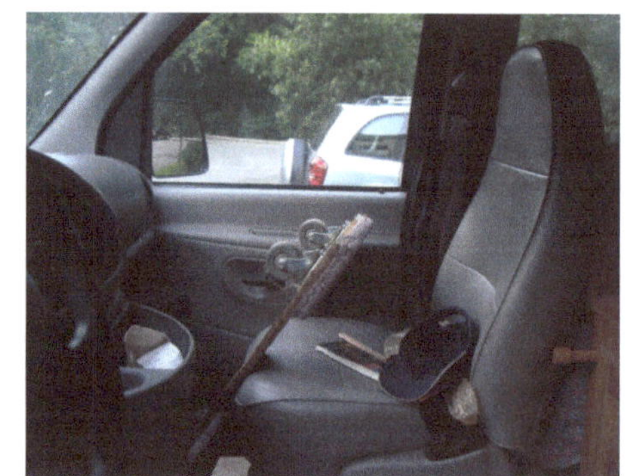

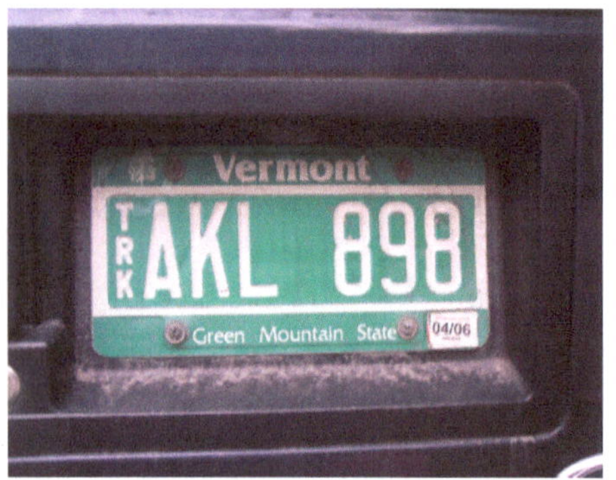

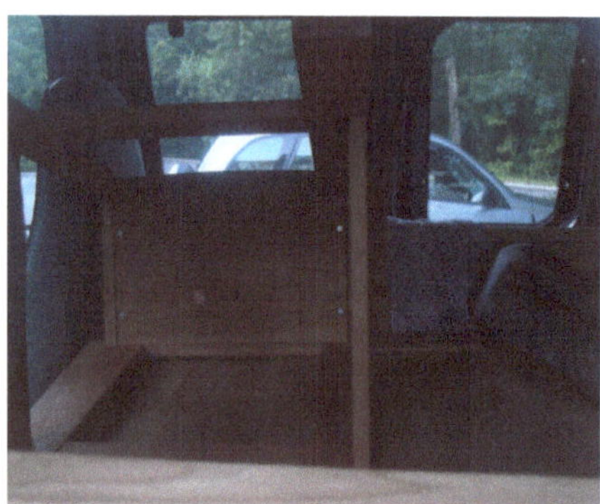

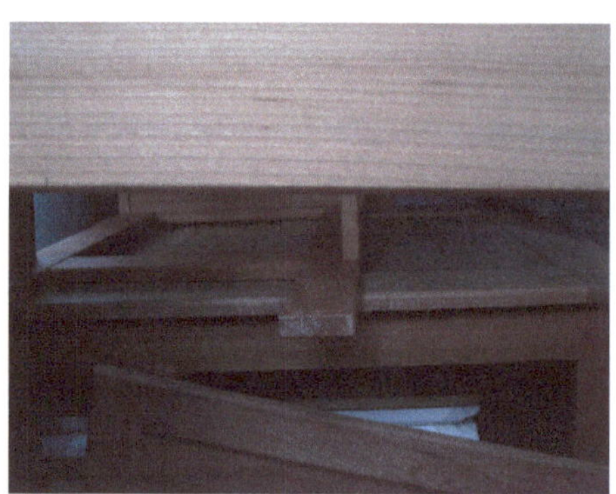

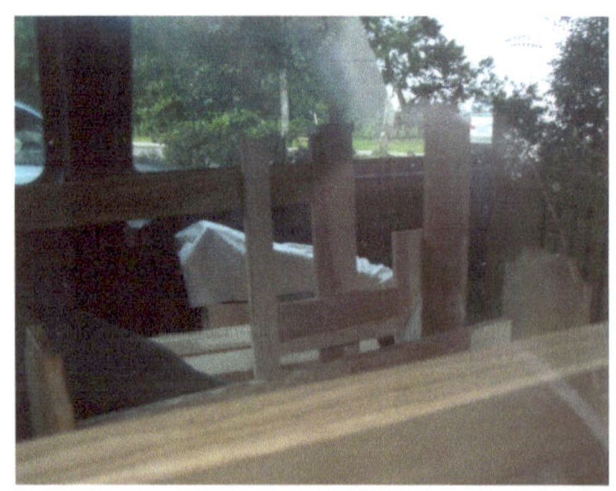

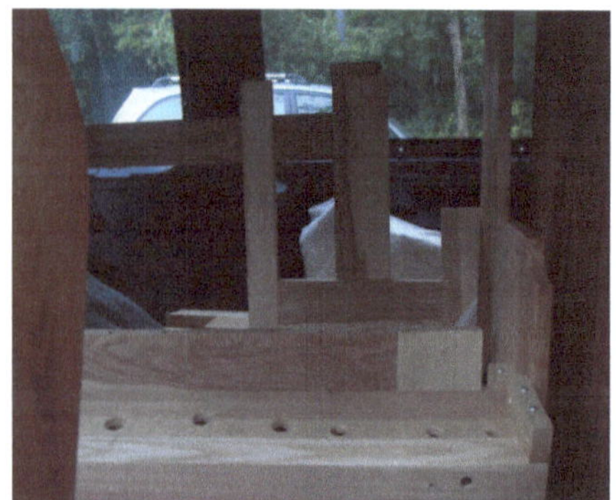

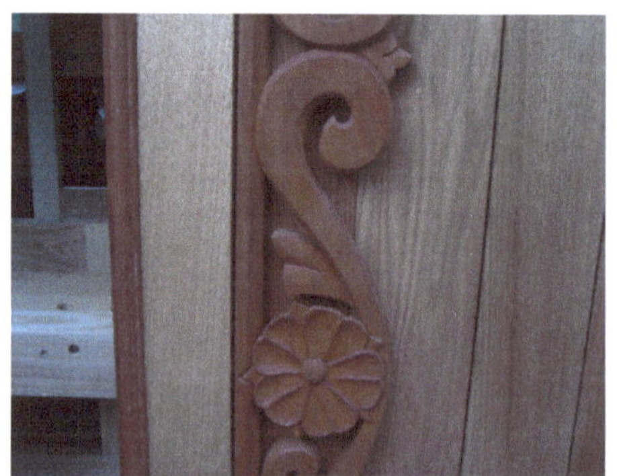

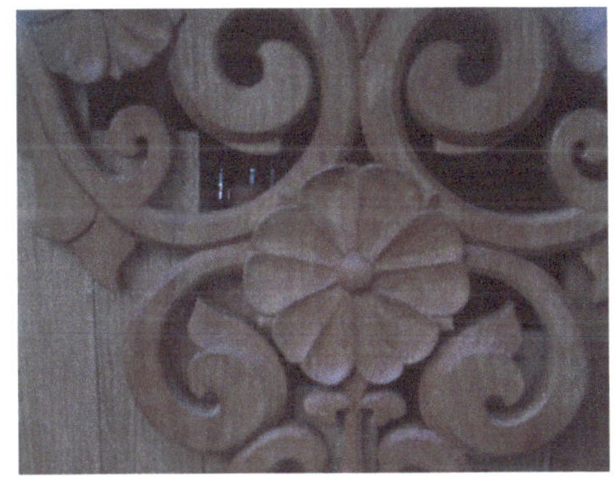
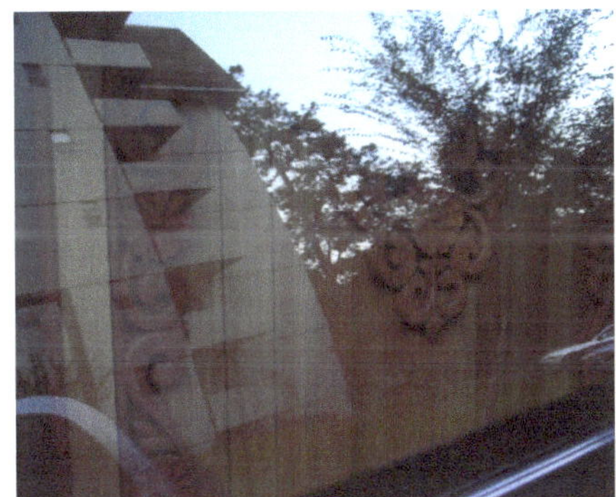
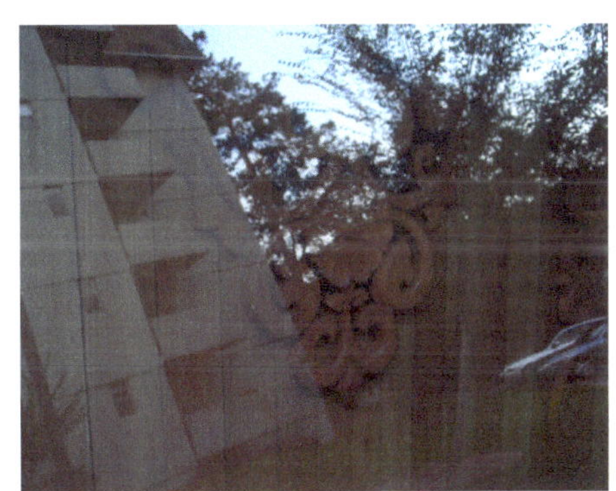
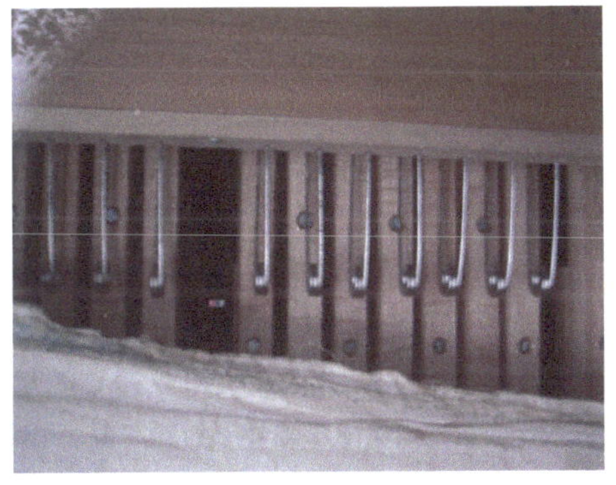
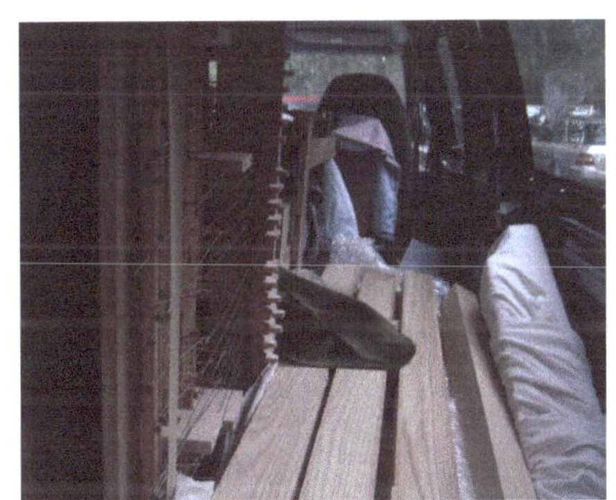
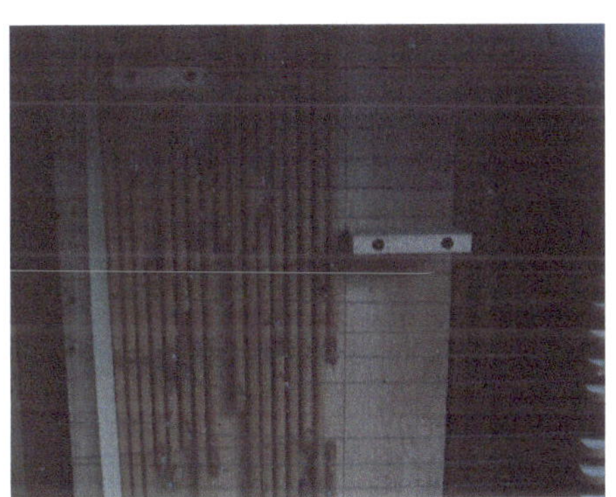
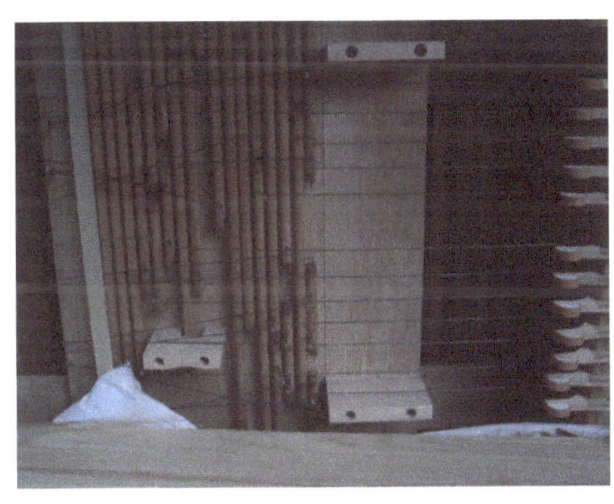
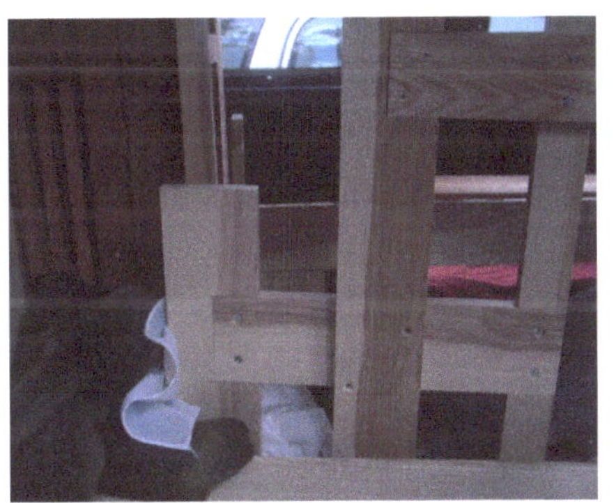
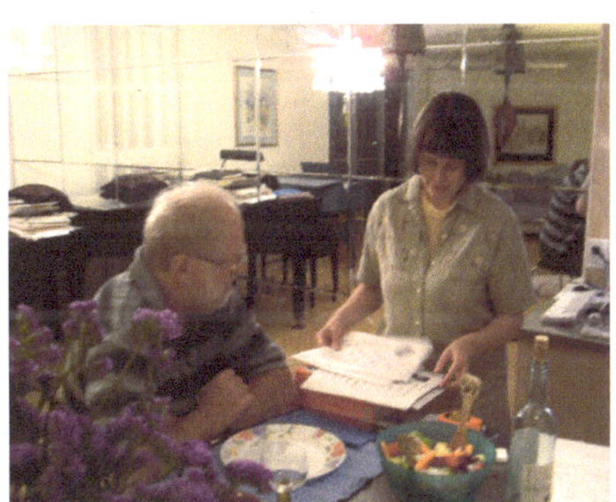

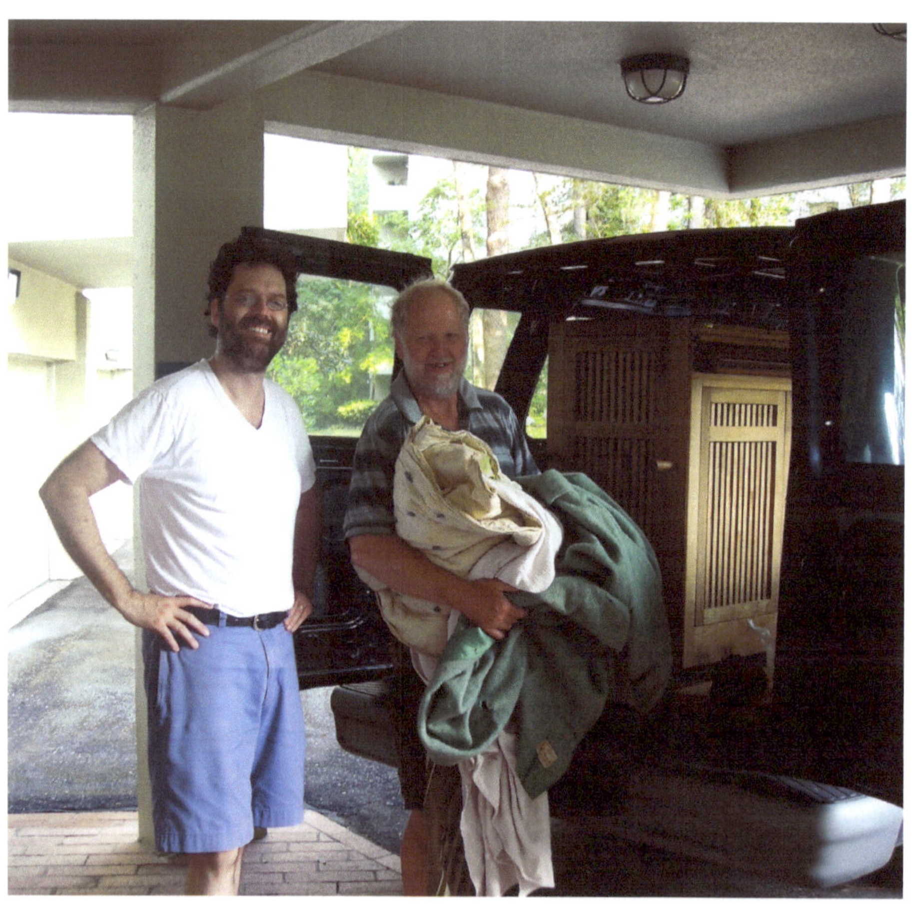

Unloading Emily in the morning of July 27, 2005. Mikesch is on the left, David Moore in the middle with the blankets, Emily on the right, still in David's delivery van.

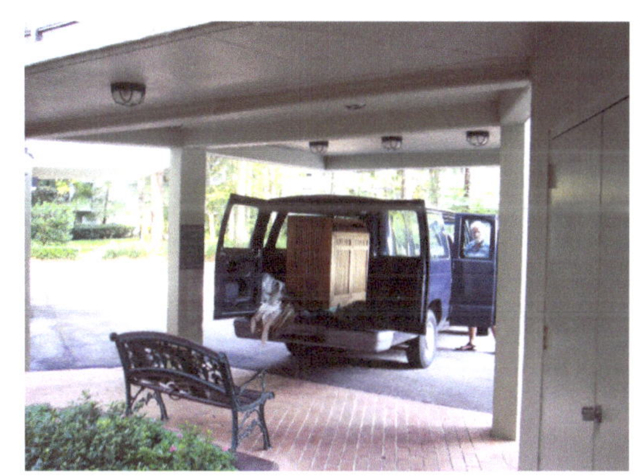

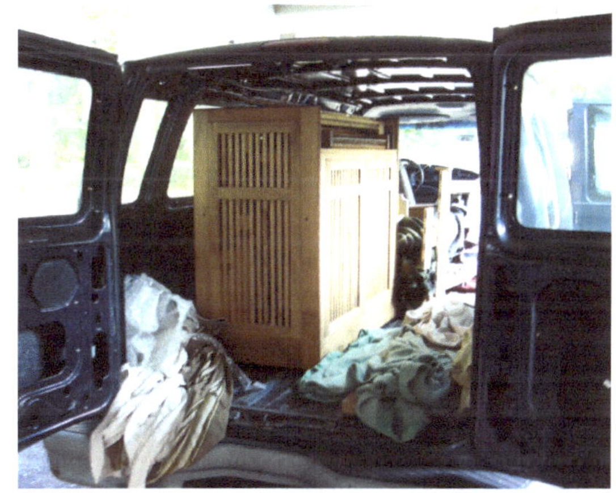

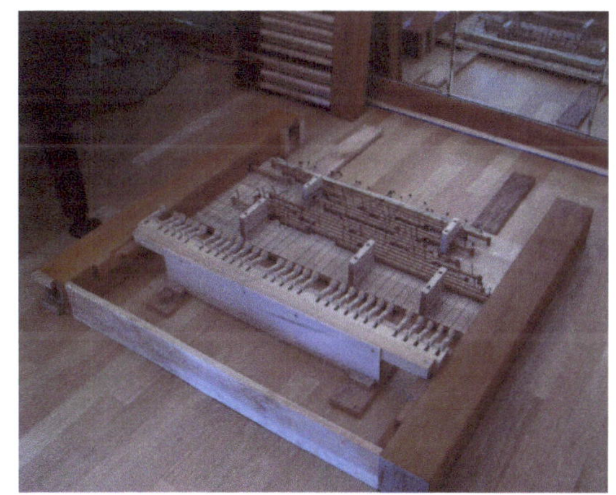

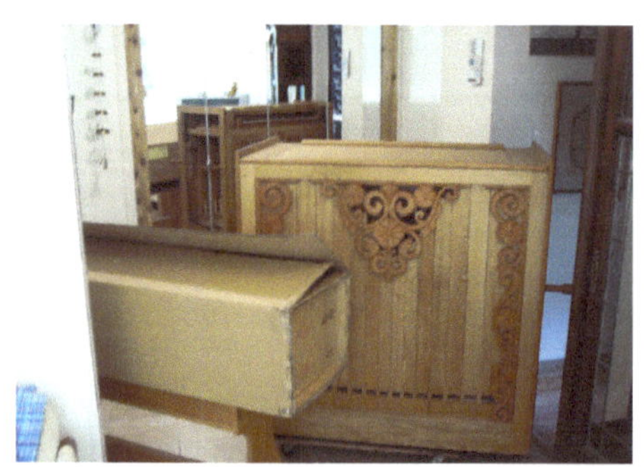

Pieces of Emily are laid out in the living room. The main organ sits in the hallway, the blower box is to the left of the couch, and the pedal pipe chest sits to the right.

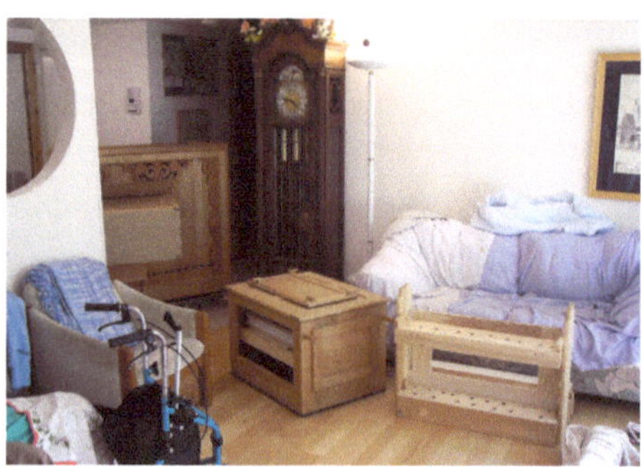

A first view into the 'city' of pipes.

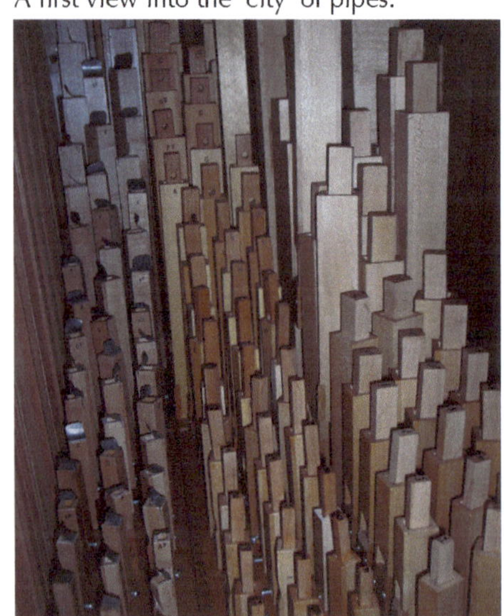

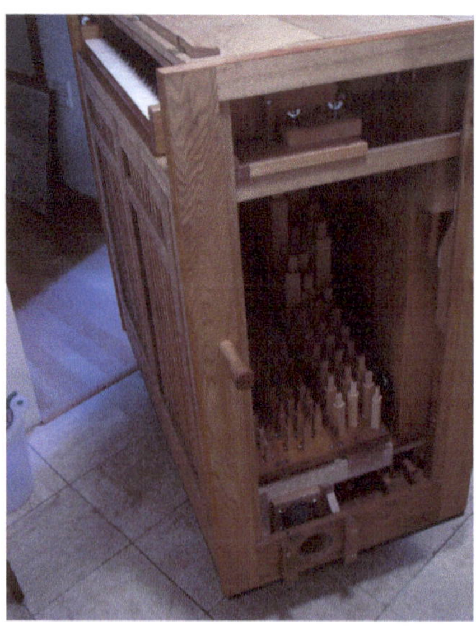

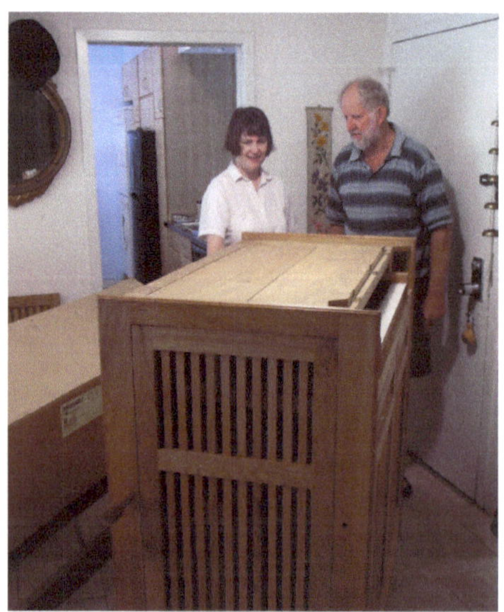

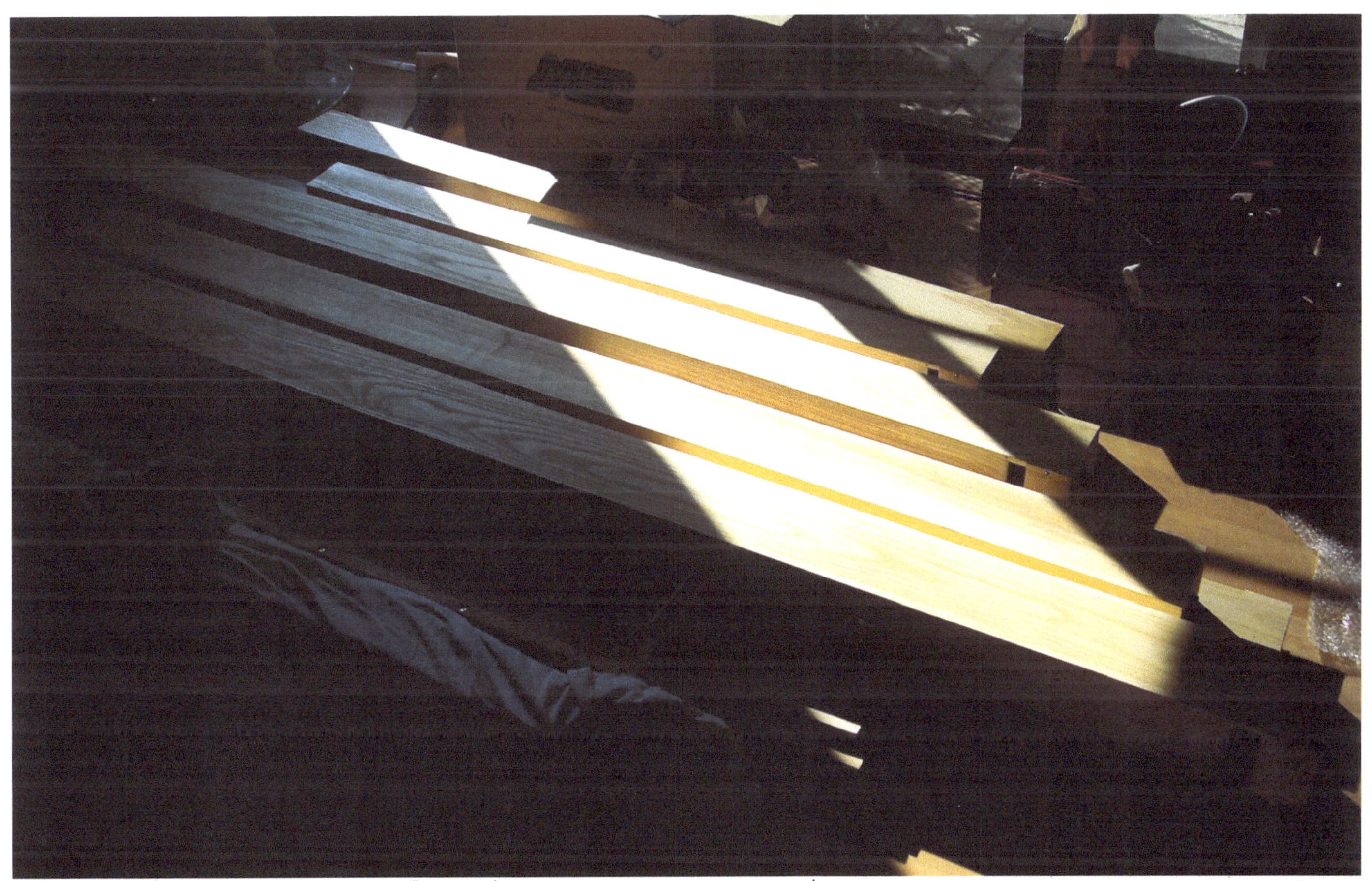
The pedal pipes rest on the living room floor in the morning sun, waiting to speak.

Assembly and Installation

On the morning of July 31, 2005 we began to assemble the organ in our living room. David told us where to put the pieces, then began to connect the different parts of the instrument. At the end of the day David was ready to do the final tuning (he had done the pre-tuning in his workshop in Vermont), Miriam had the chance to play Emily for the first time, with a big smile on her face....

For samples of Emily's voice, please go online to http://www.iwclib.org

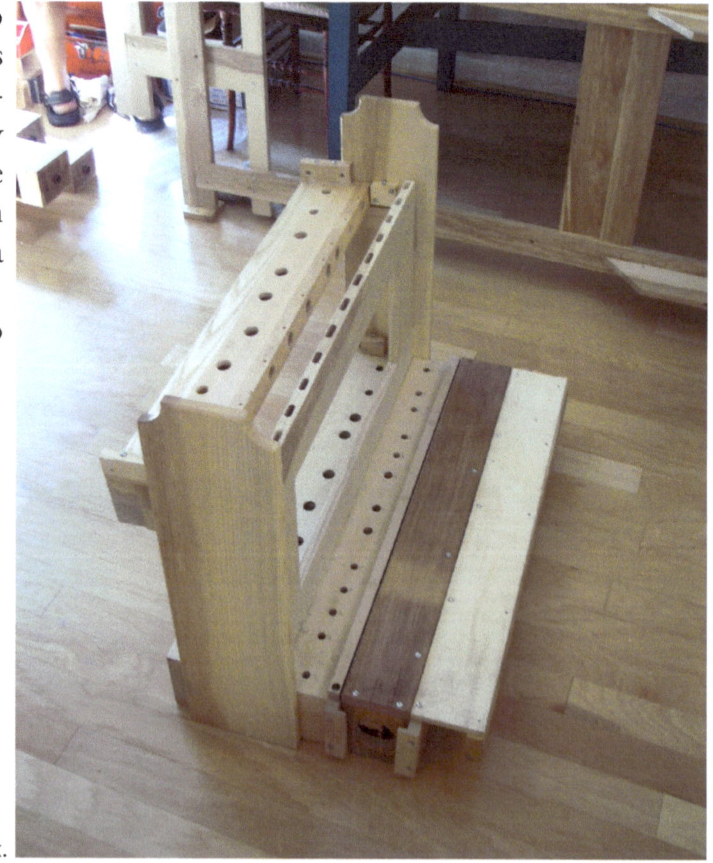

Emily's pedal rack.

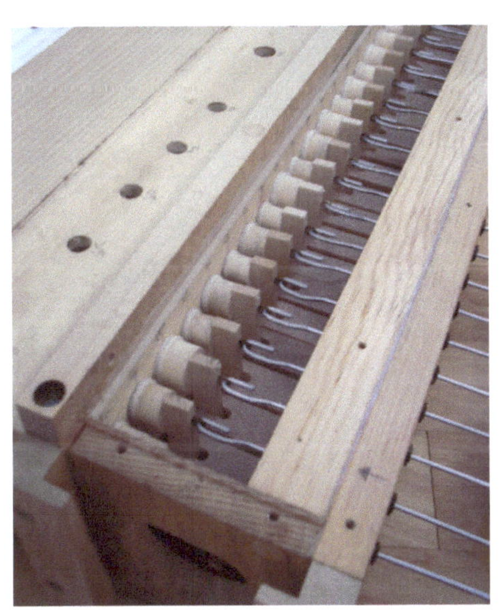

Pedal roller board and action.

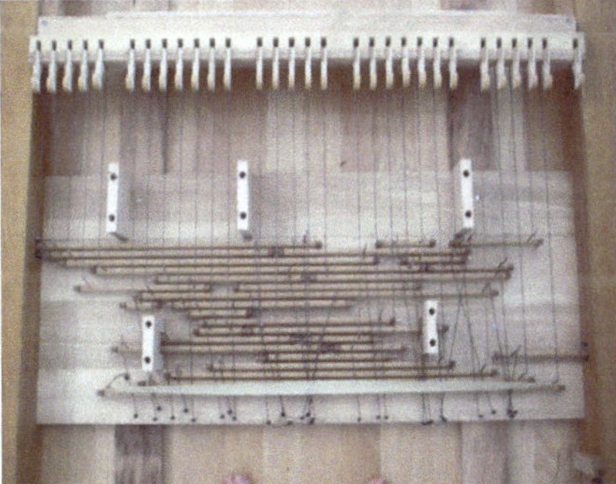

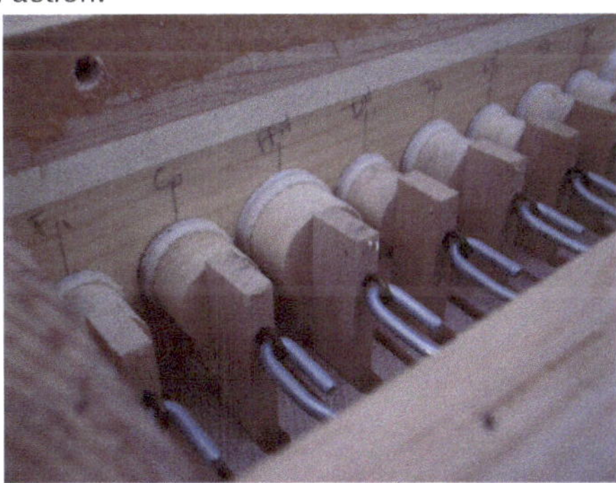

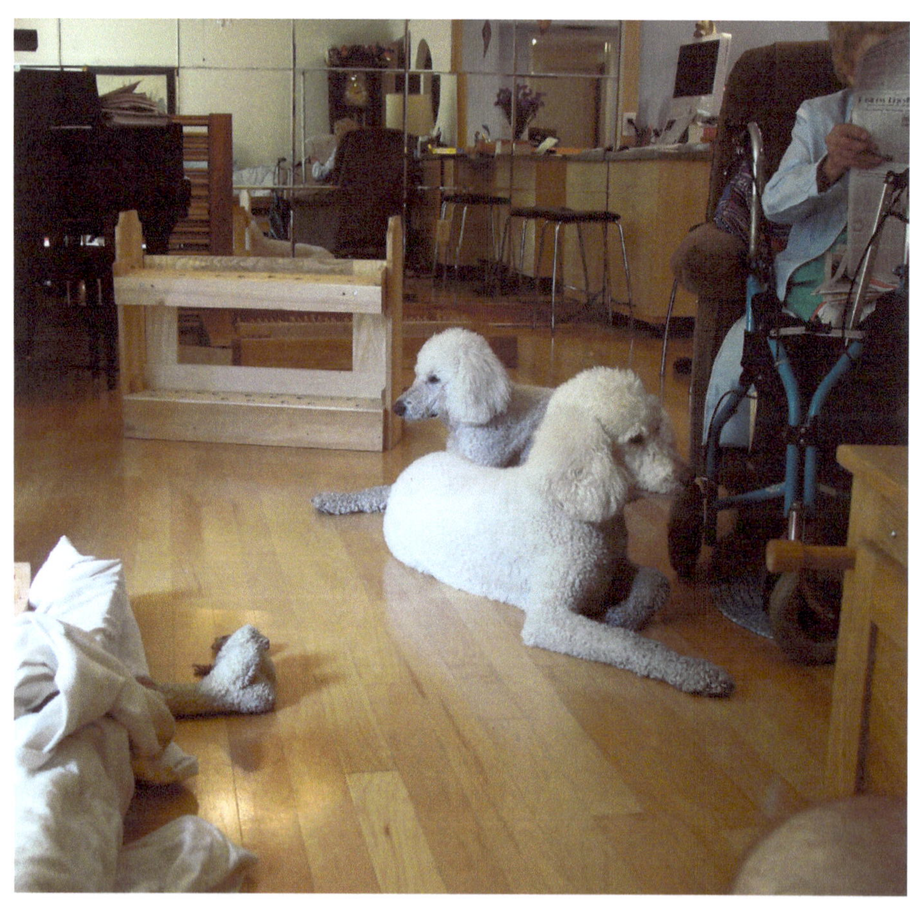

Even poodle cousins Lambchop and Zsa Zsa are in a relaxed mode of meditation, waiting for Emily to sing her first notes.

Closeup of pedal roller board.

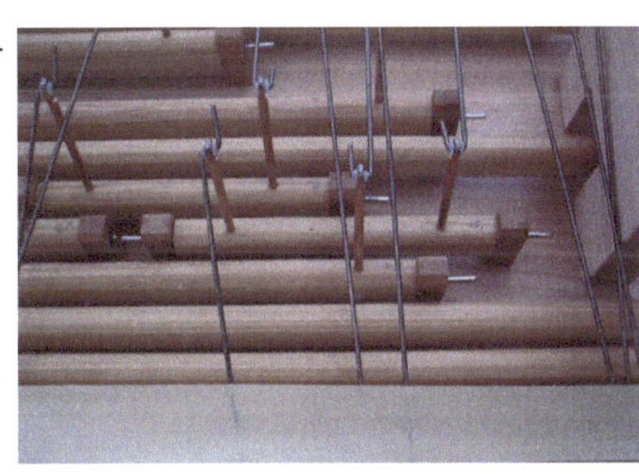

Mechanical pedal pipe action (and Mikesch' feet as scale).

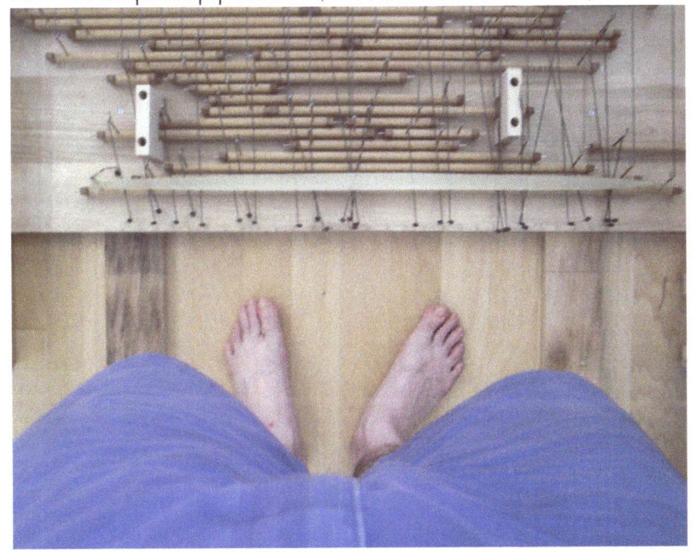

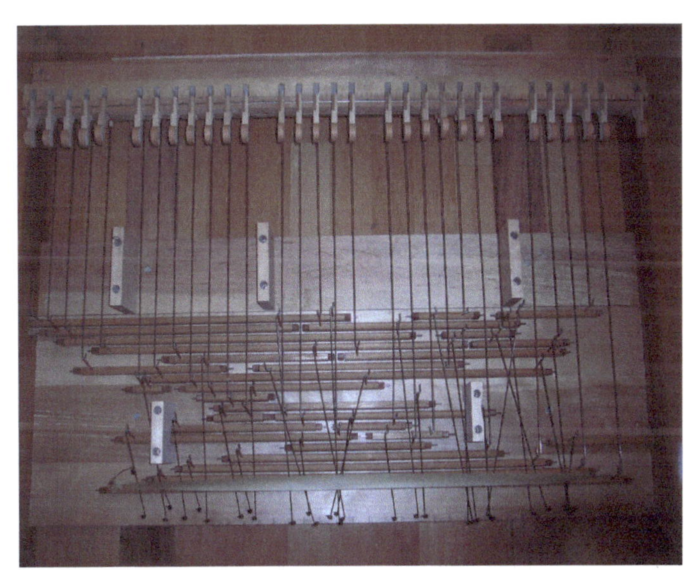

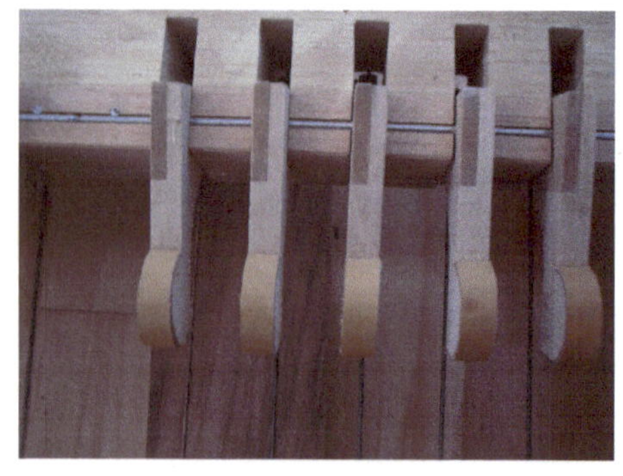

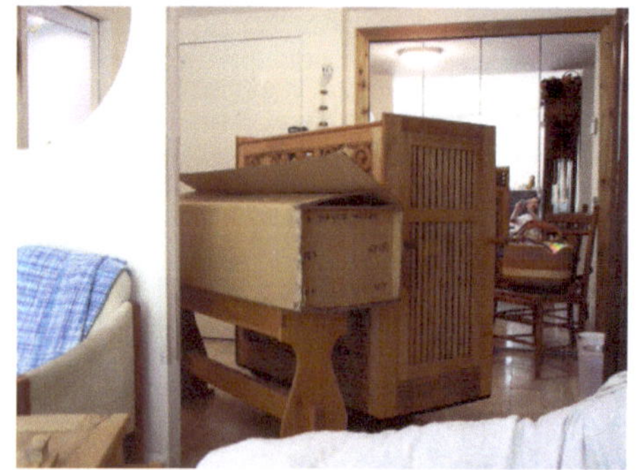

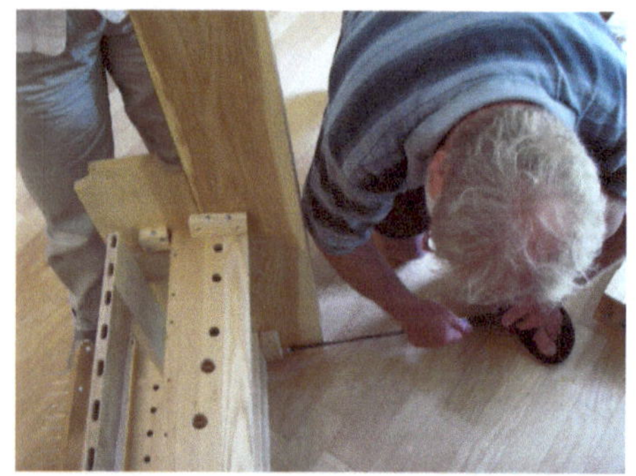

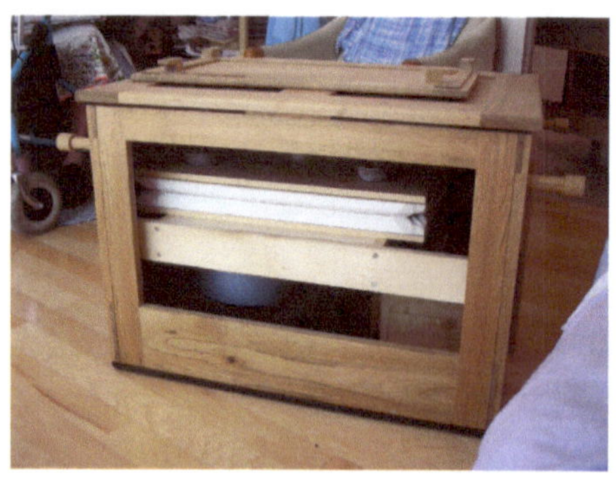

Blower motor box.

Wind conduit for pedal pipes.

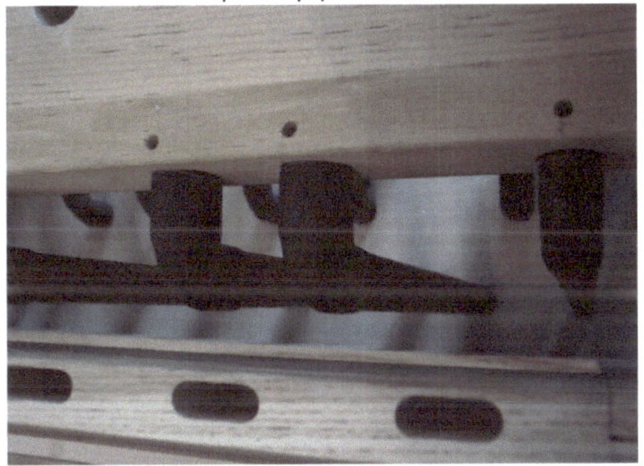

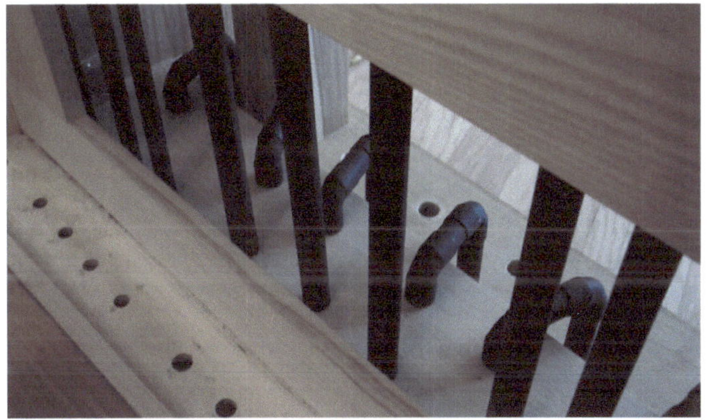

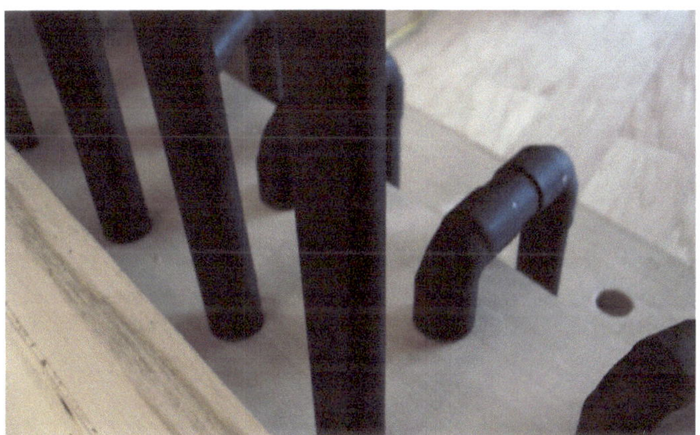

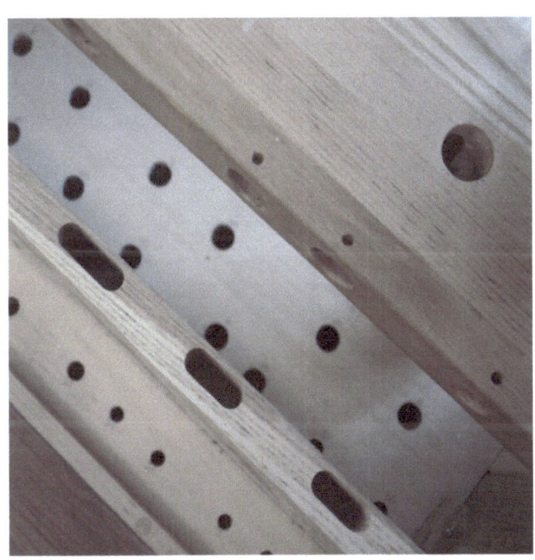

Pedal pipe toe board.

David Moore's sacred blanket-o-screws, a different screw for any occasion...

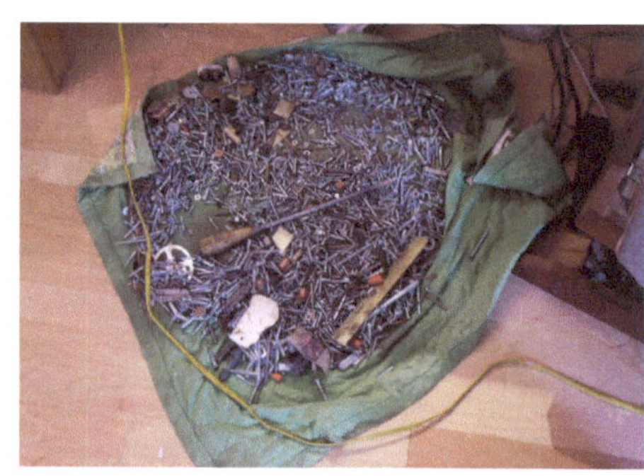

Pedal pipe rack installation.

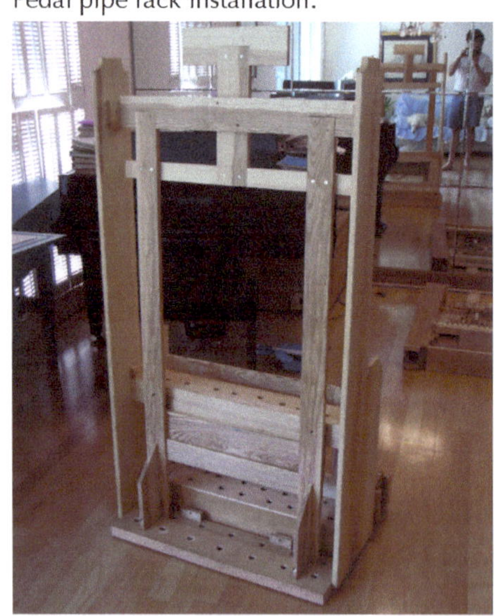

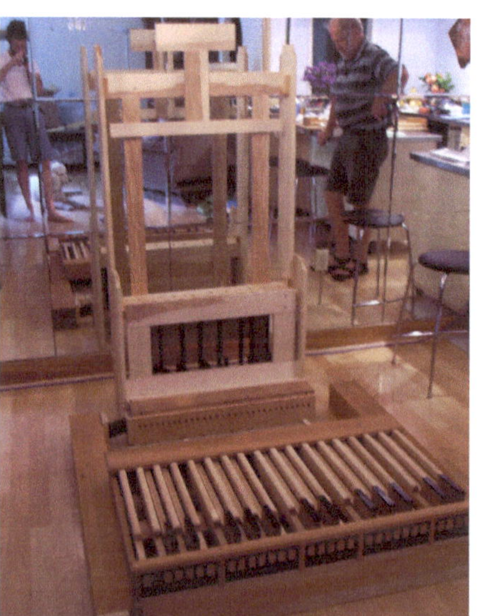

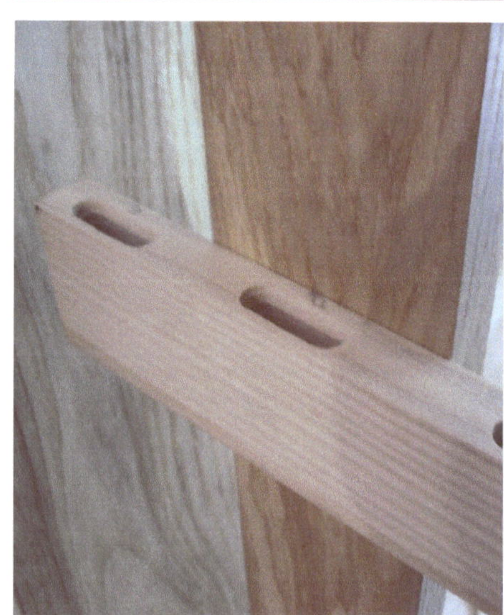

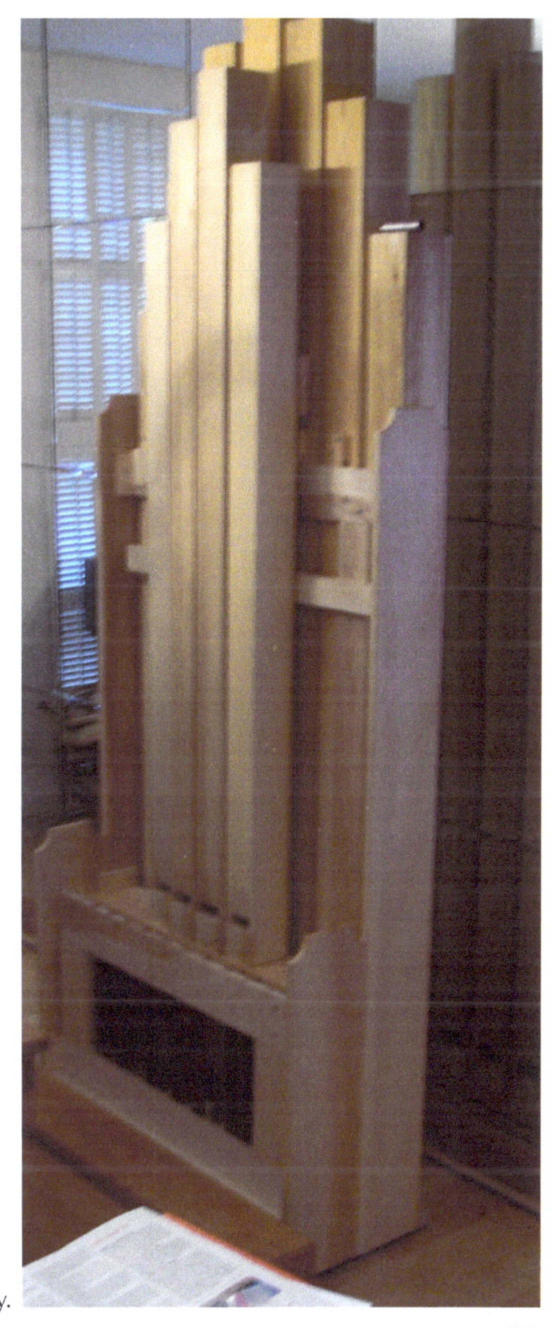

Pedal pipe assembly.

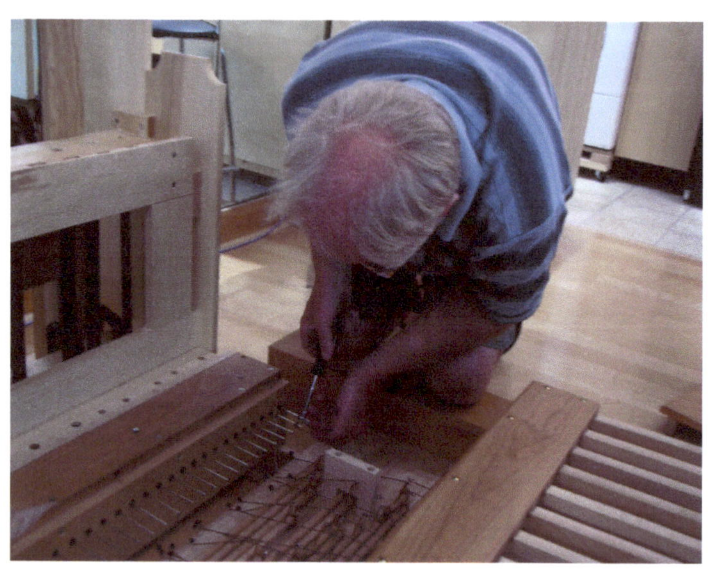

Installation of pedal pipe action.

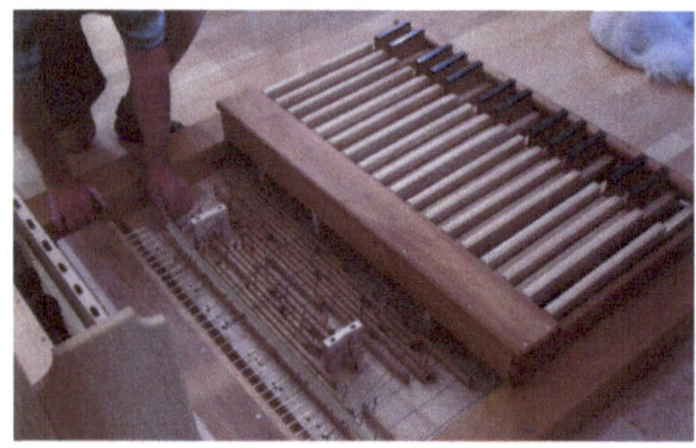

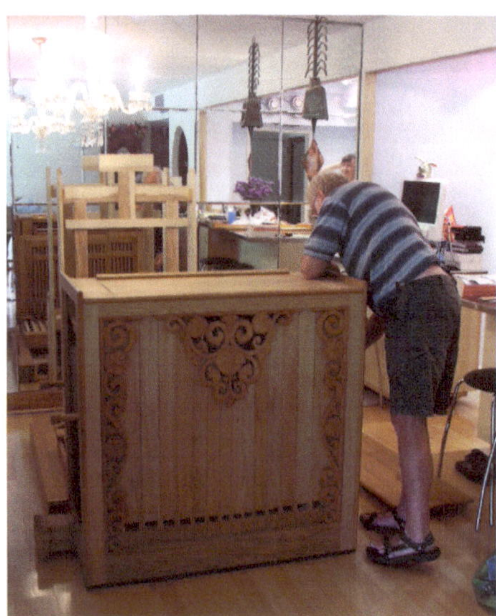

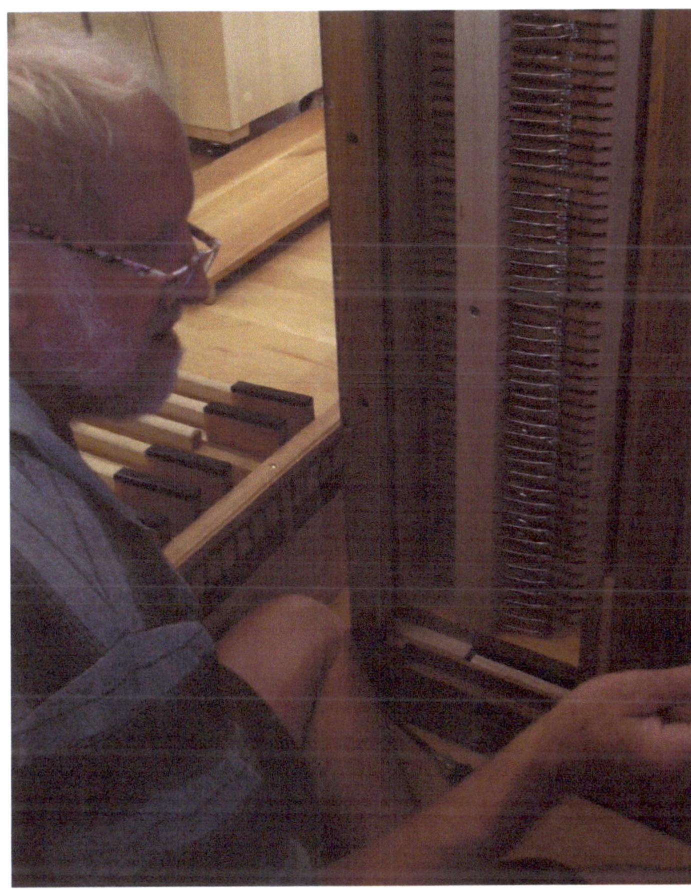

David Moore working on the 'bumboard', showing keyboard action at bottom of organ chest (organ is rotated 90° on its side).

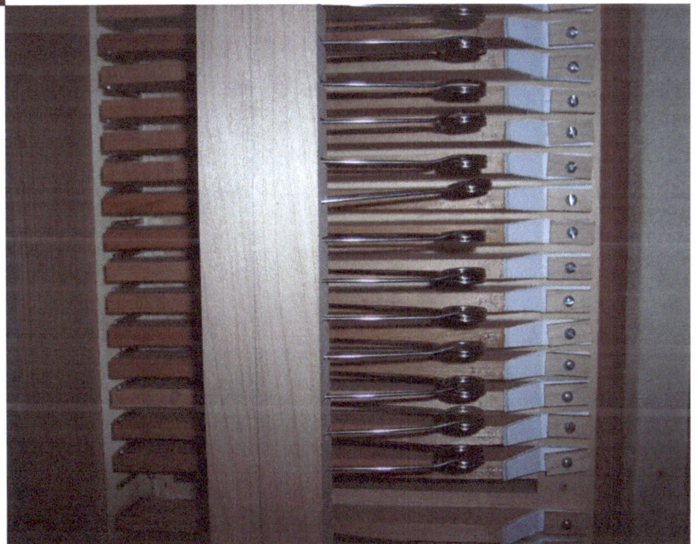

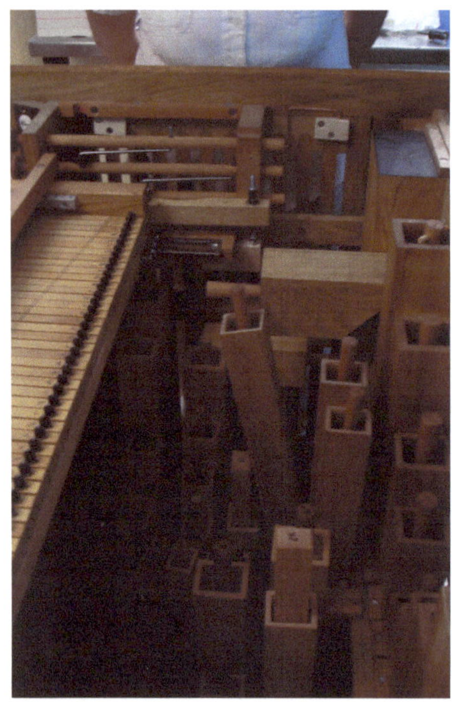

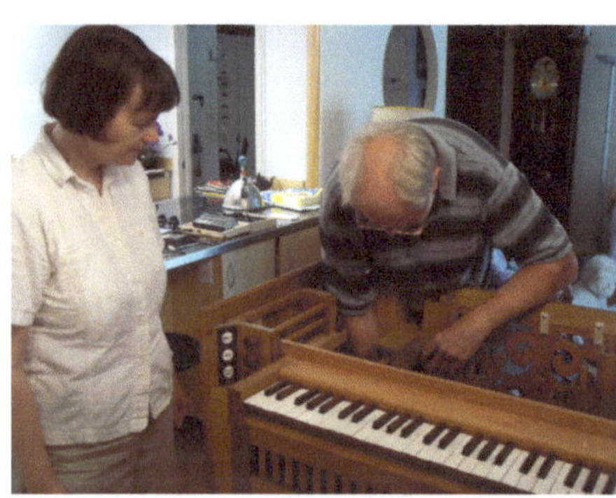

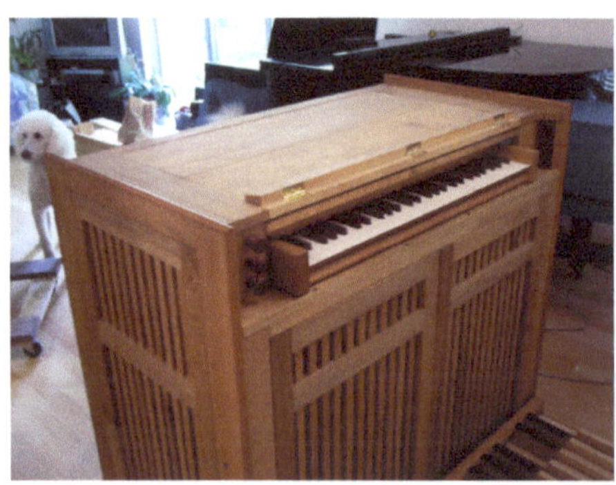

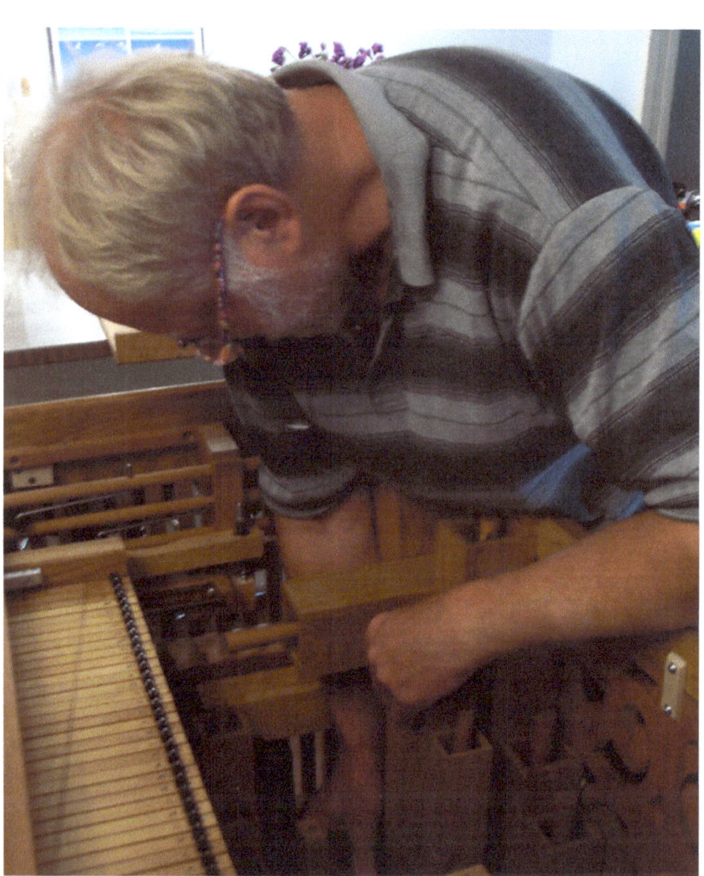

Testing the Organ

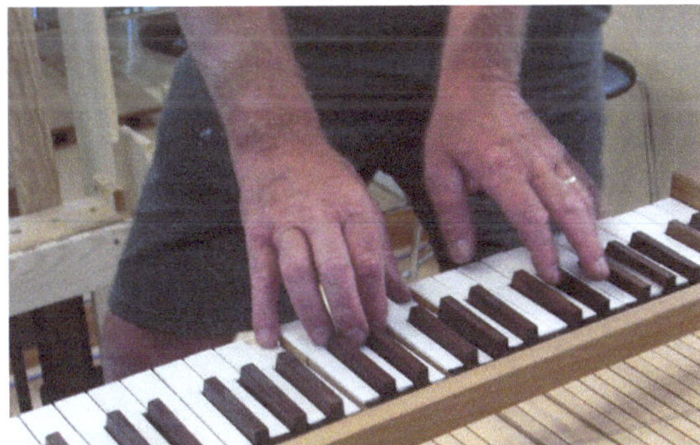

Testing key action.

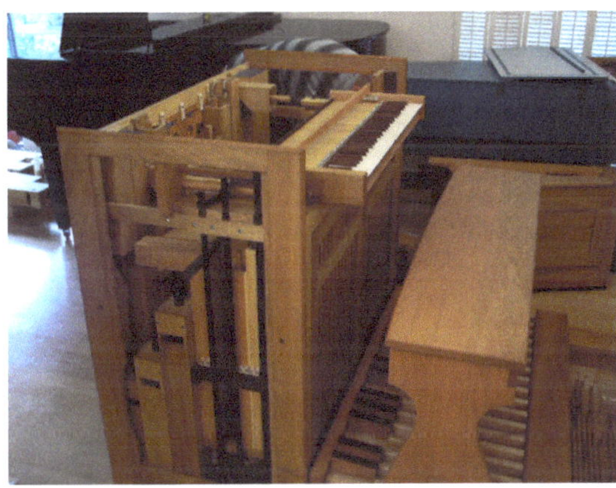

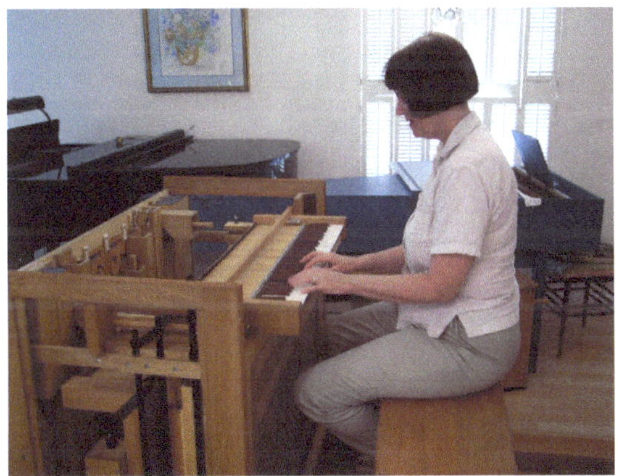

Final Tuning

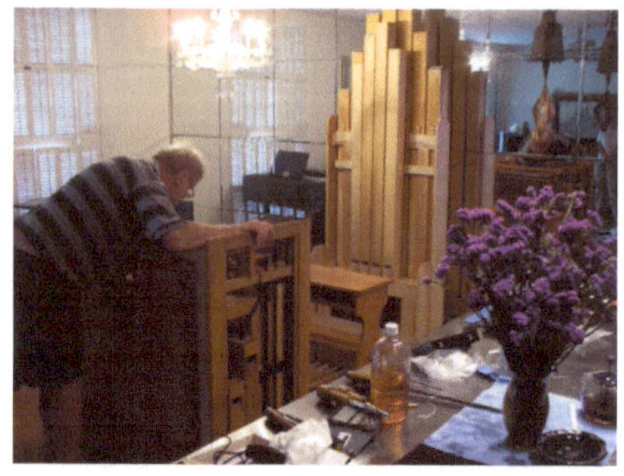

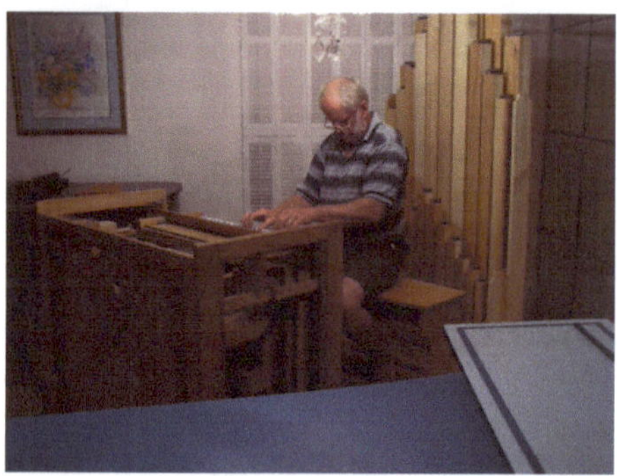

David Moore doing the final tuning (at times with an alien light-hat) using a German-made Vogel-Scheer tuner CTS-321.

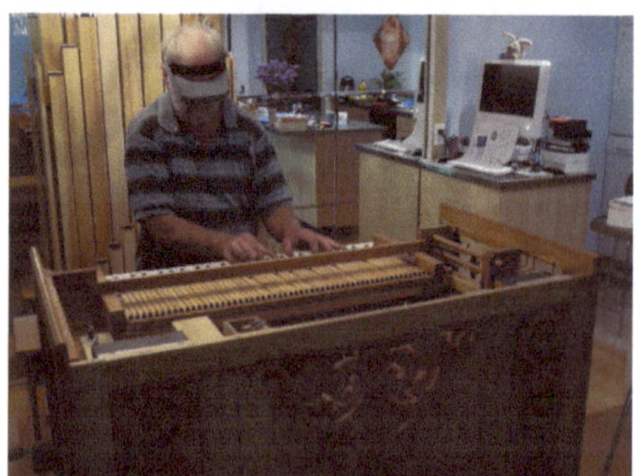

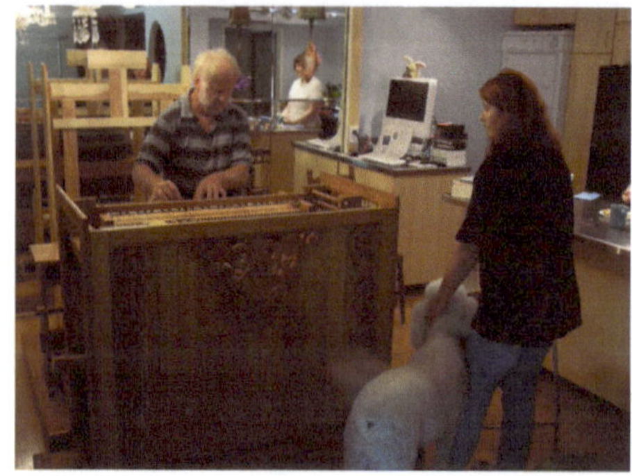

Voicing the organ.

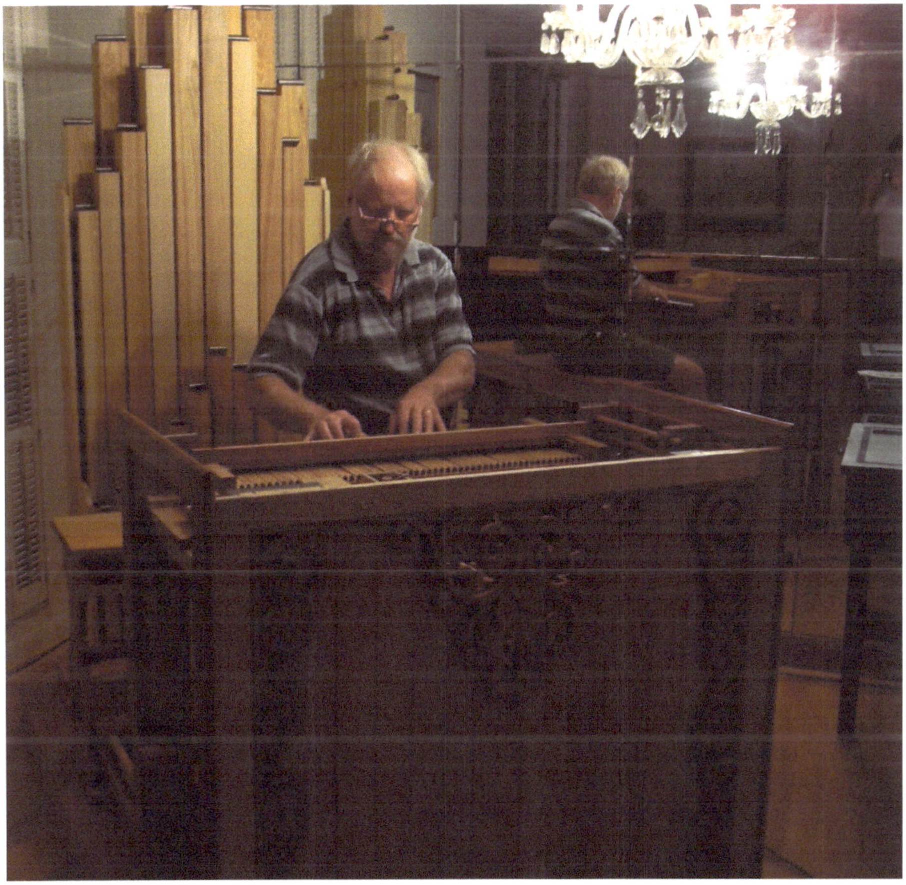

Timeline

July 29, 2005

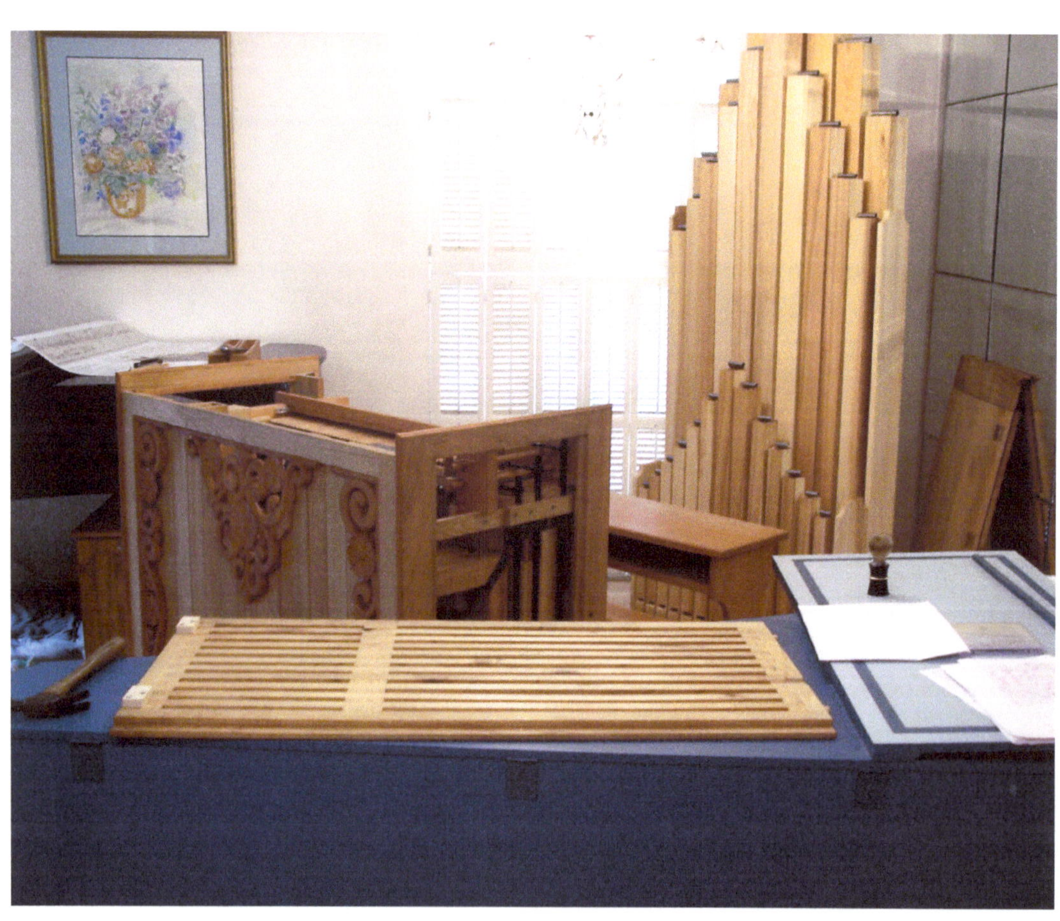

July 30, 2005

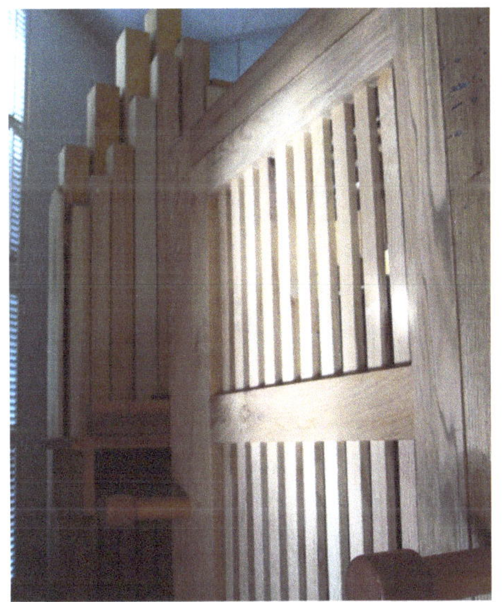

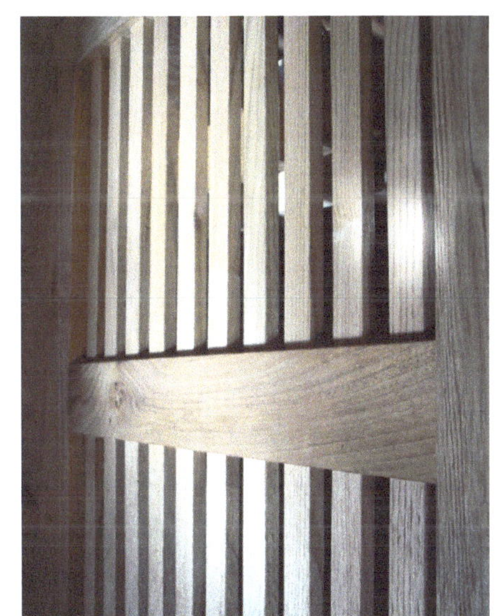

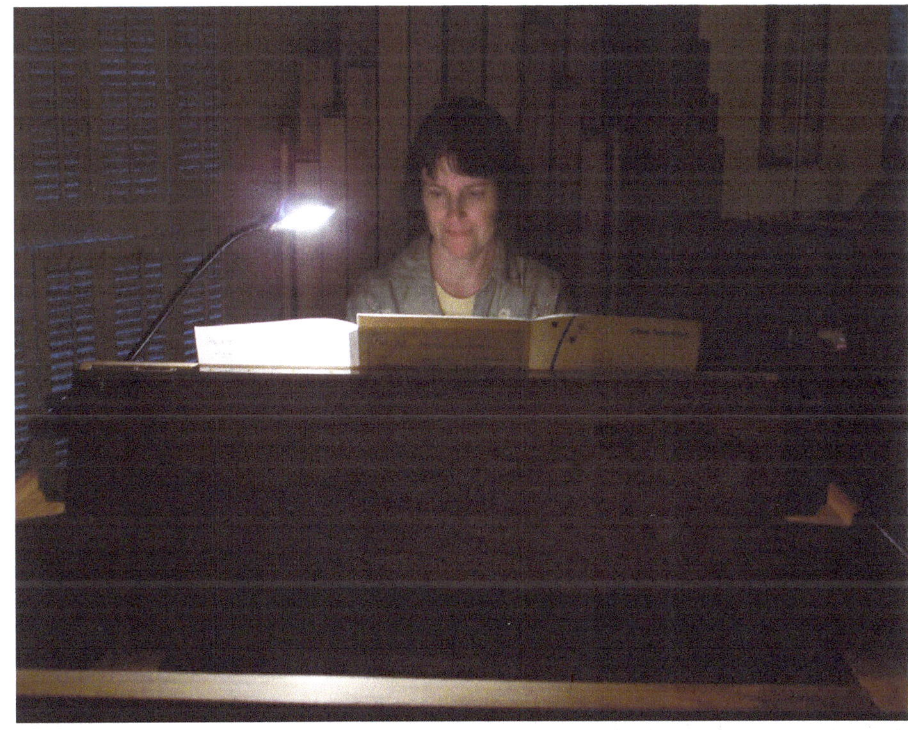

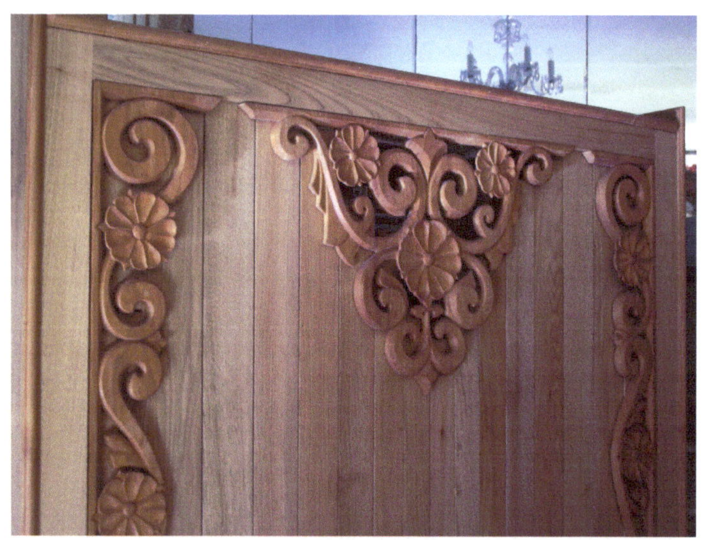

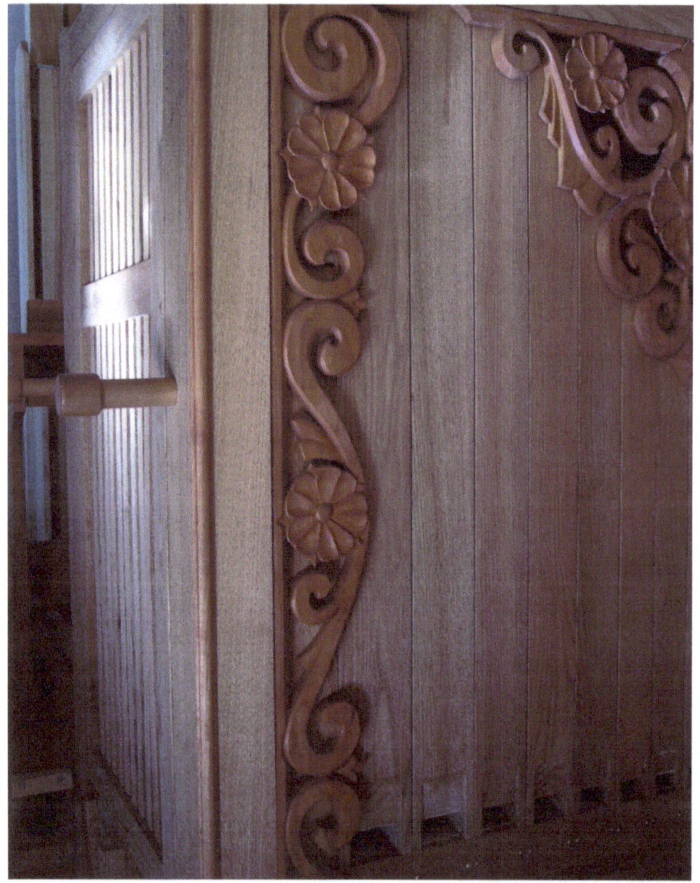

July 31, 2005

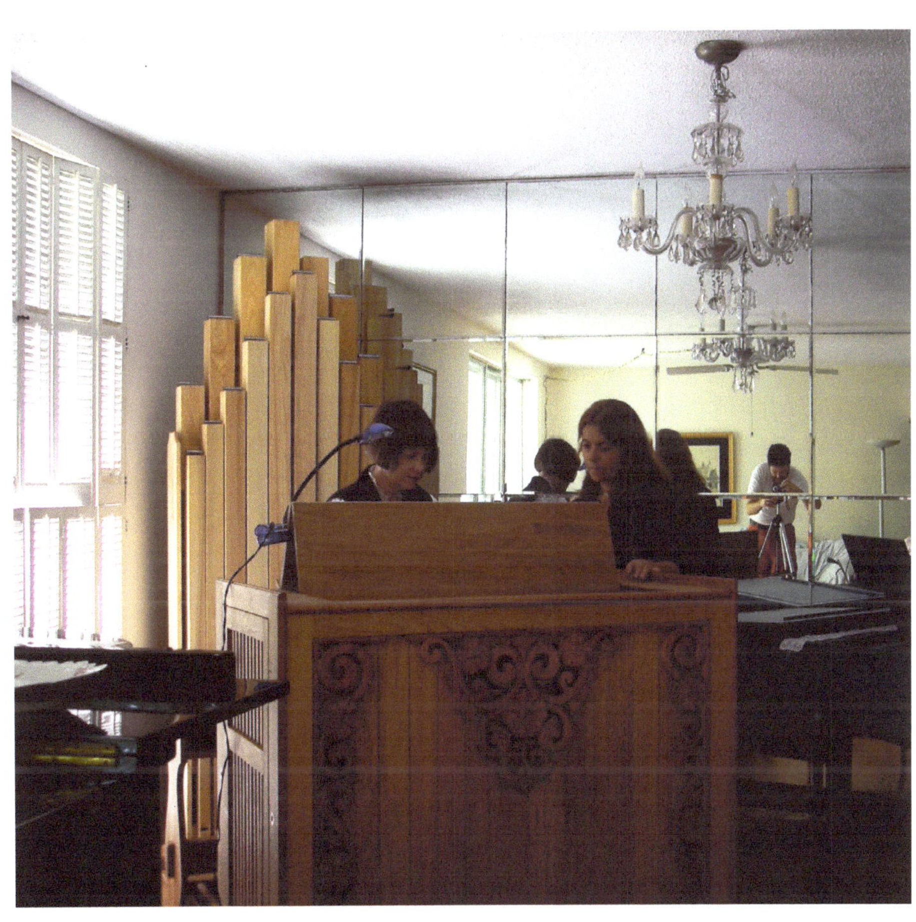

August 7, 2005

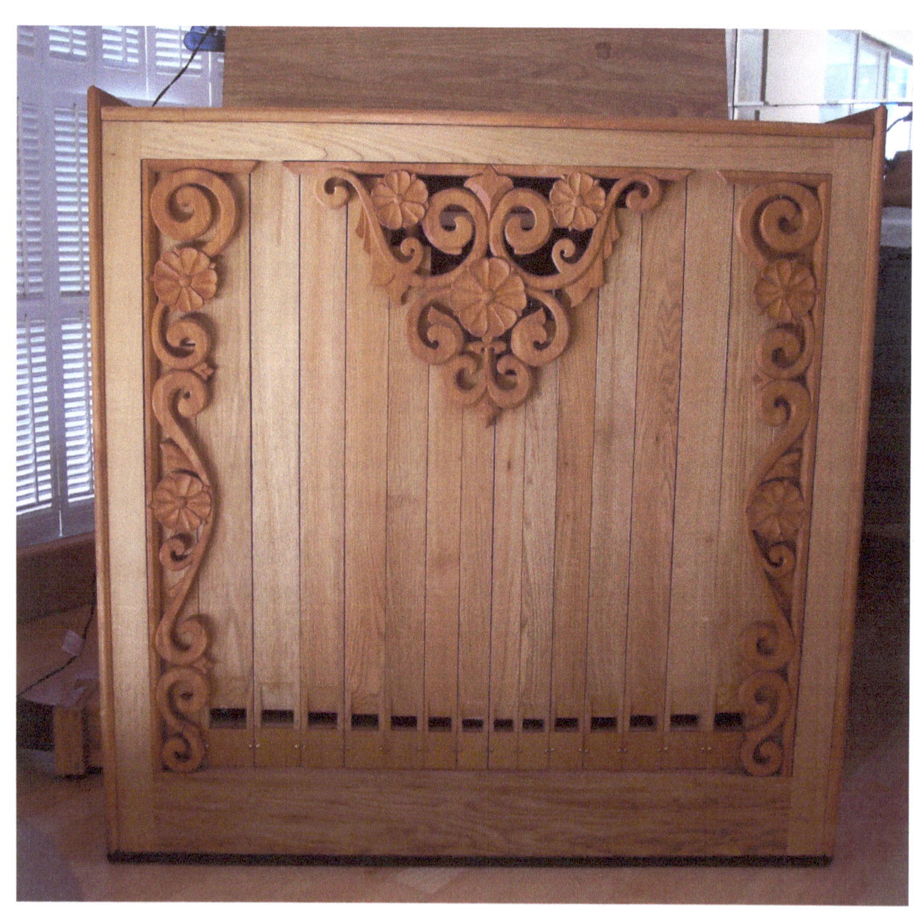

Details

Opus 28
A.D.
Moore
& Co
Pomfret
Vt.
2005

Fifteenth
Flute
Stopped
Diapason

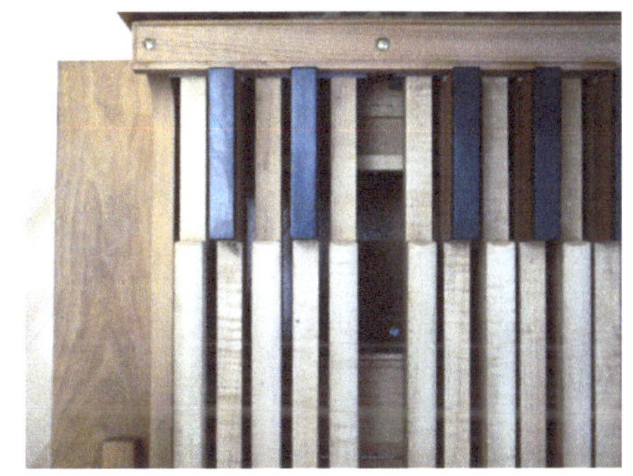

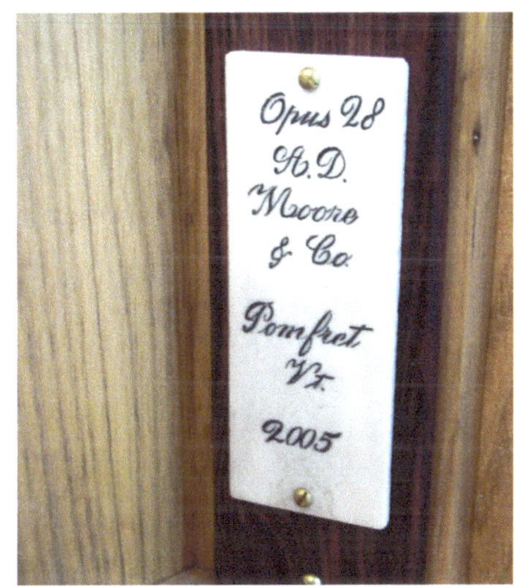

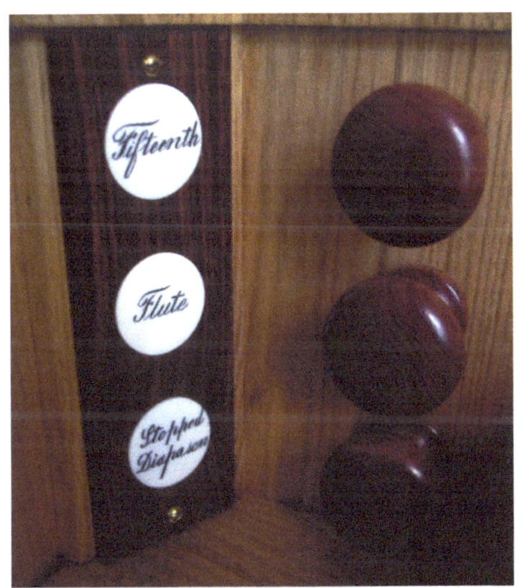

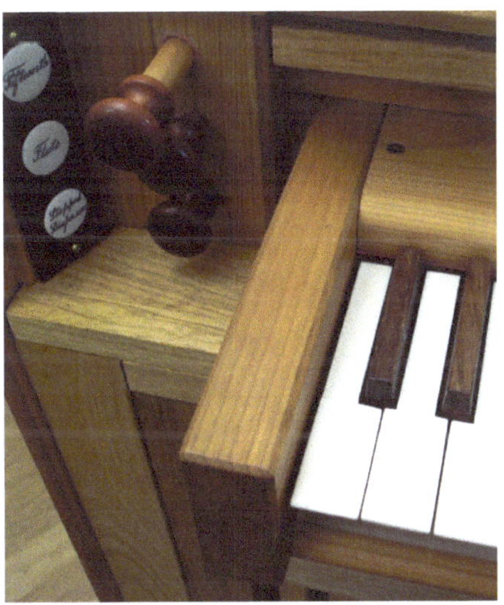

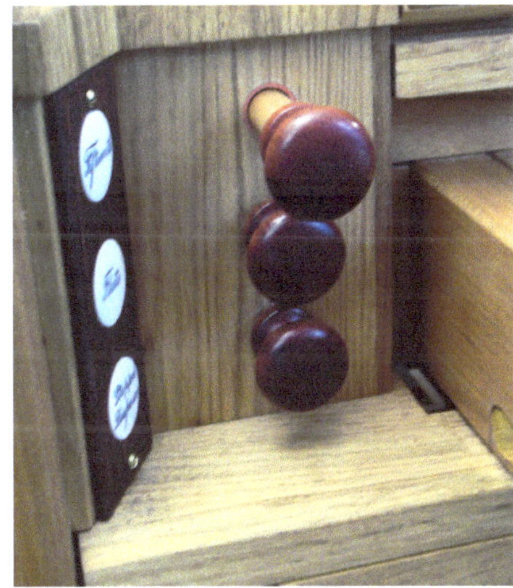

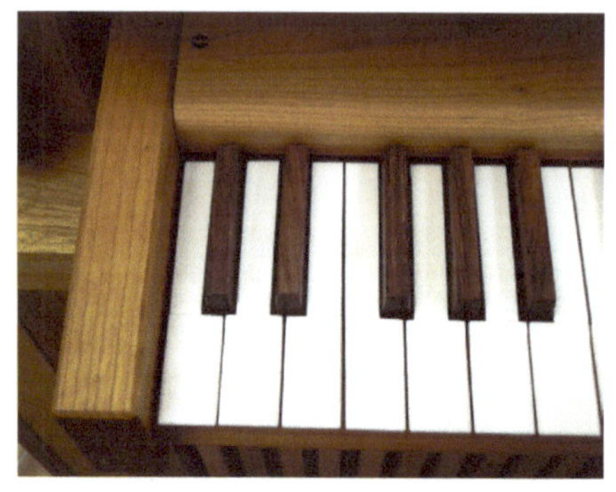

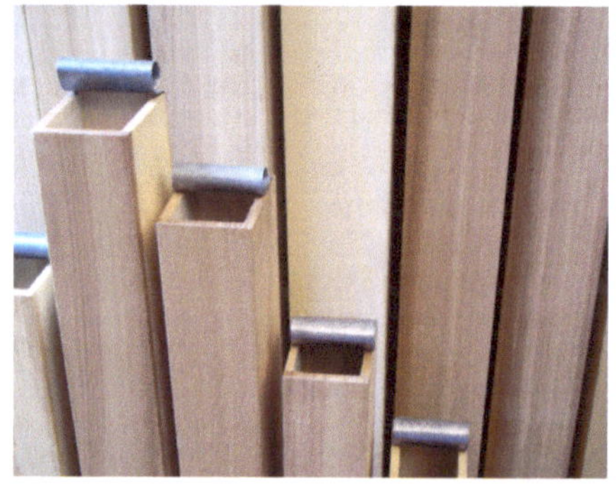

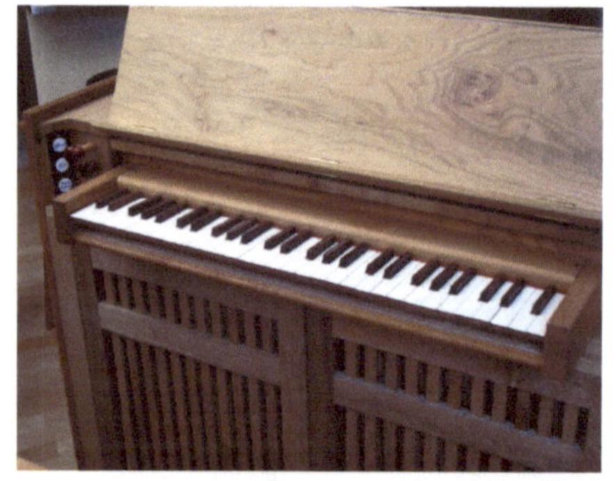

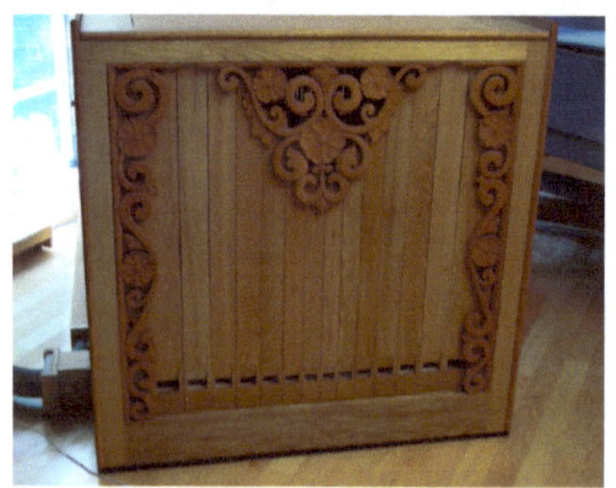

Opus 28 Emily in its final location in Miriam Zach's International Women Composers Library in Gainesville, Florida.

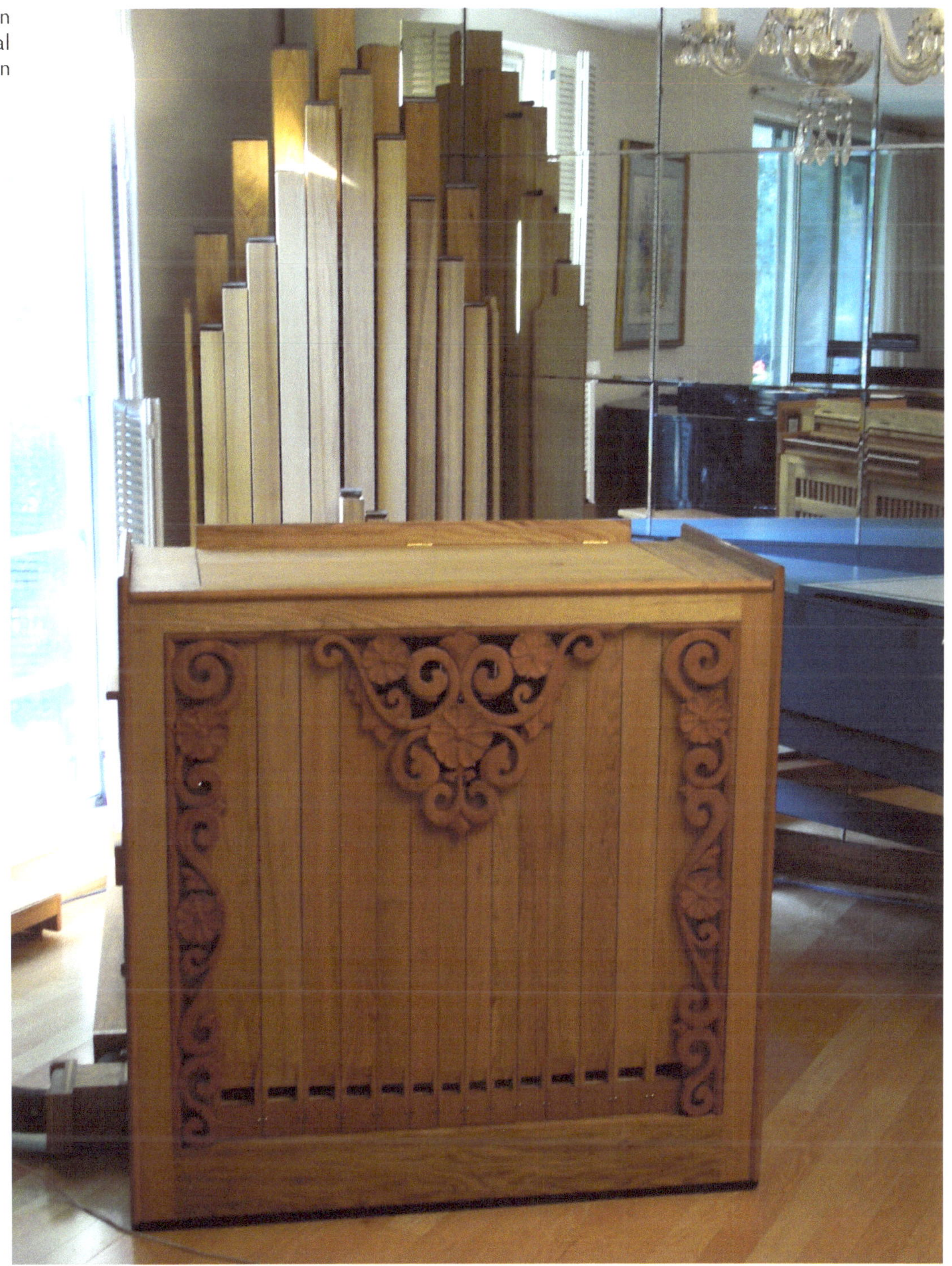

Wood Carving

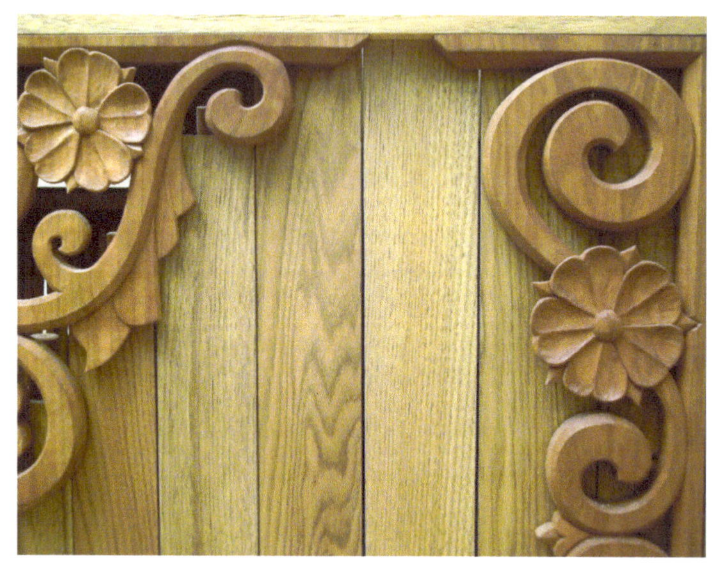

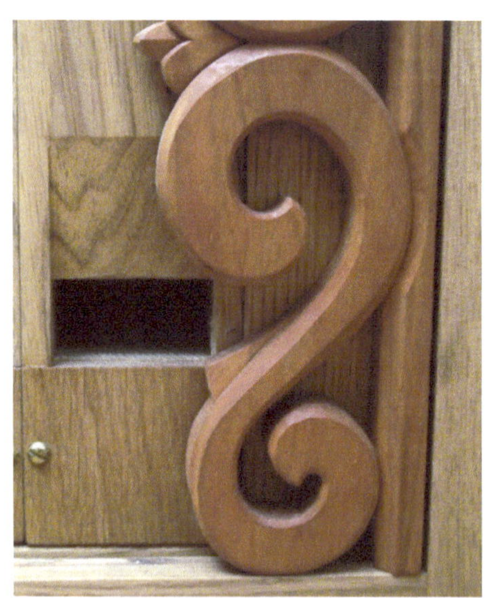

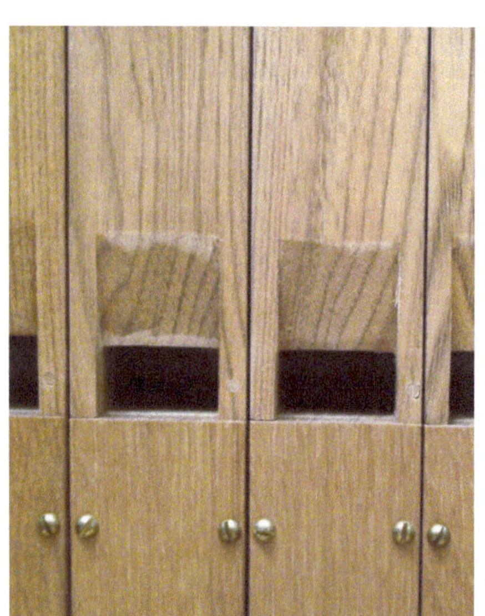

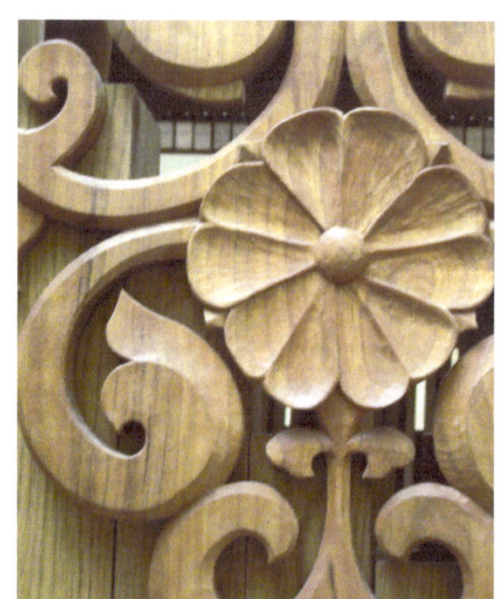

Pipes

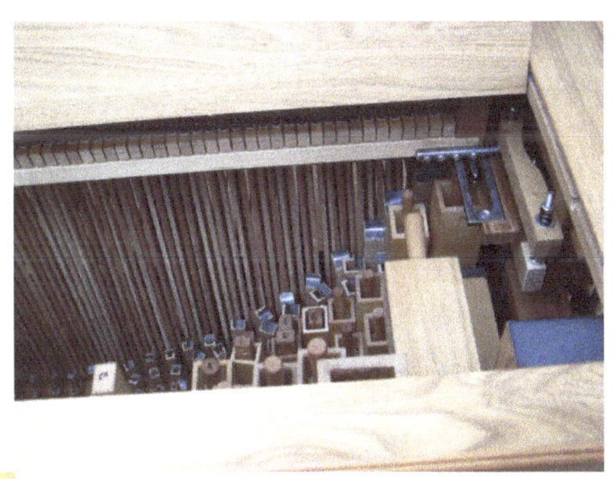

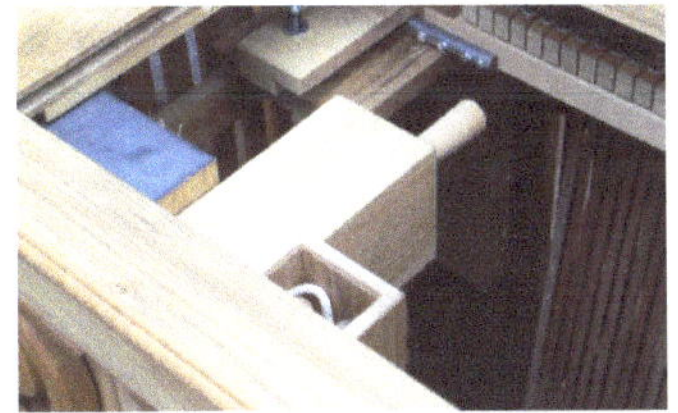

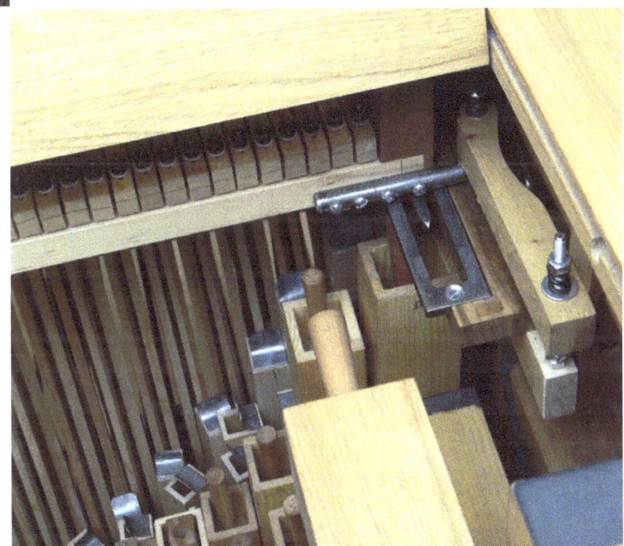

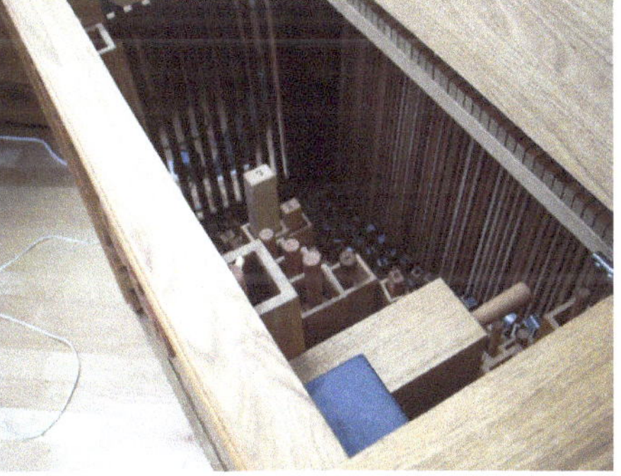

Keyboard chest pipes.

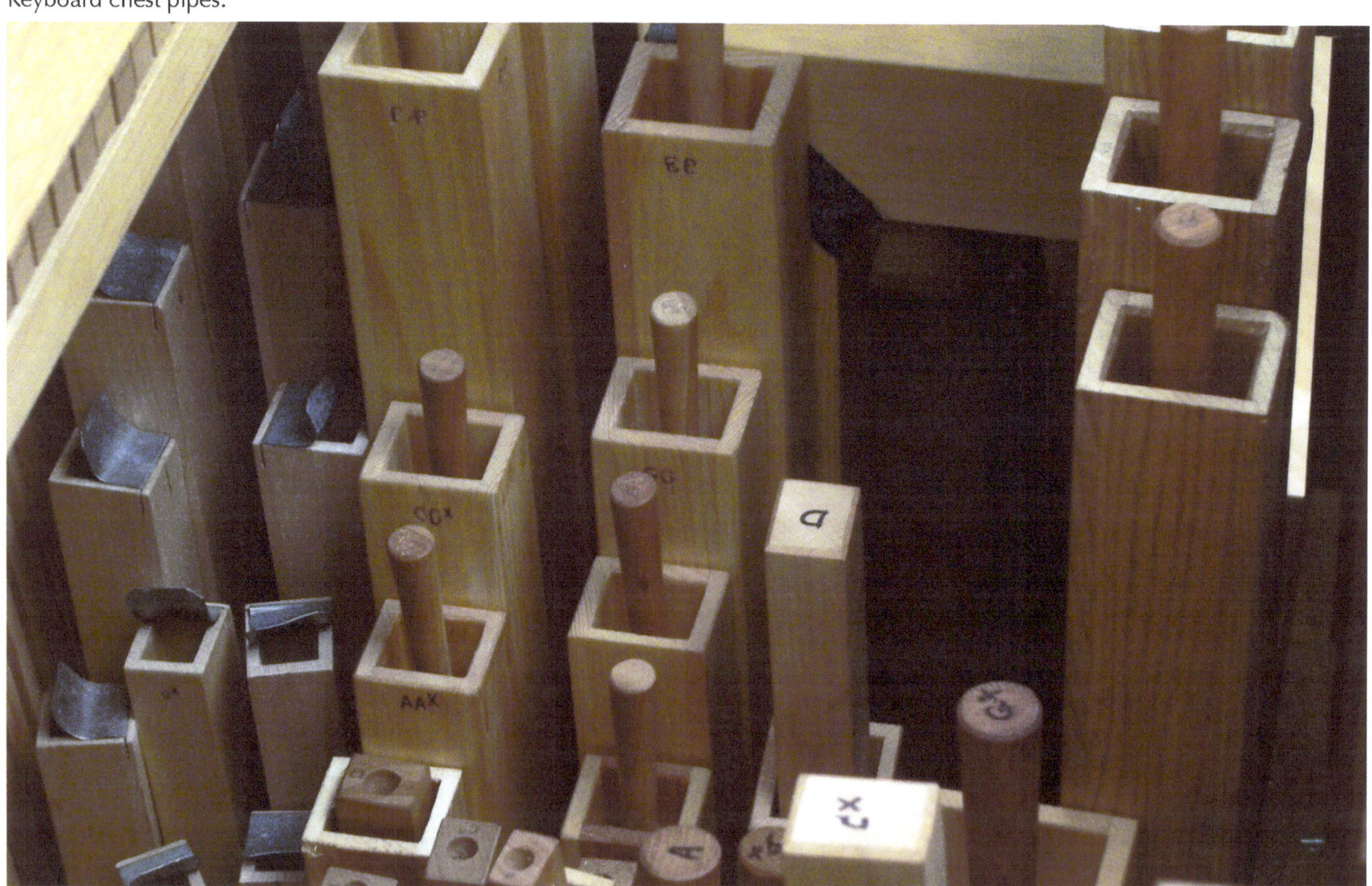

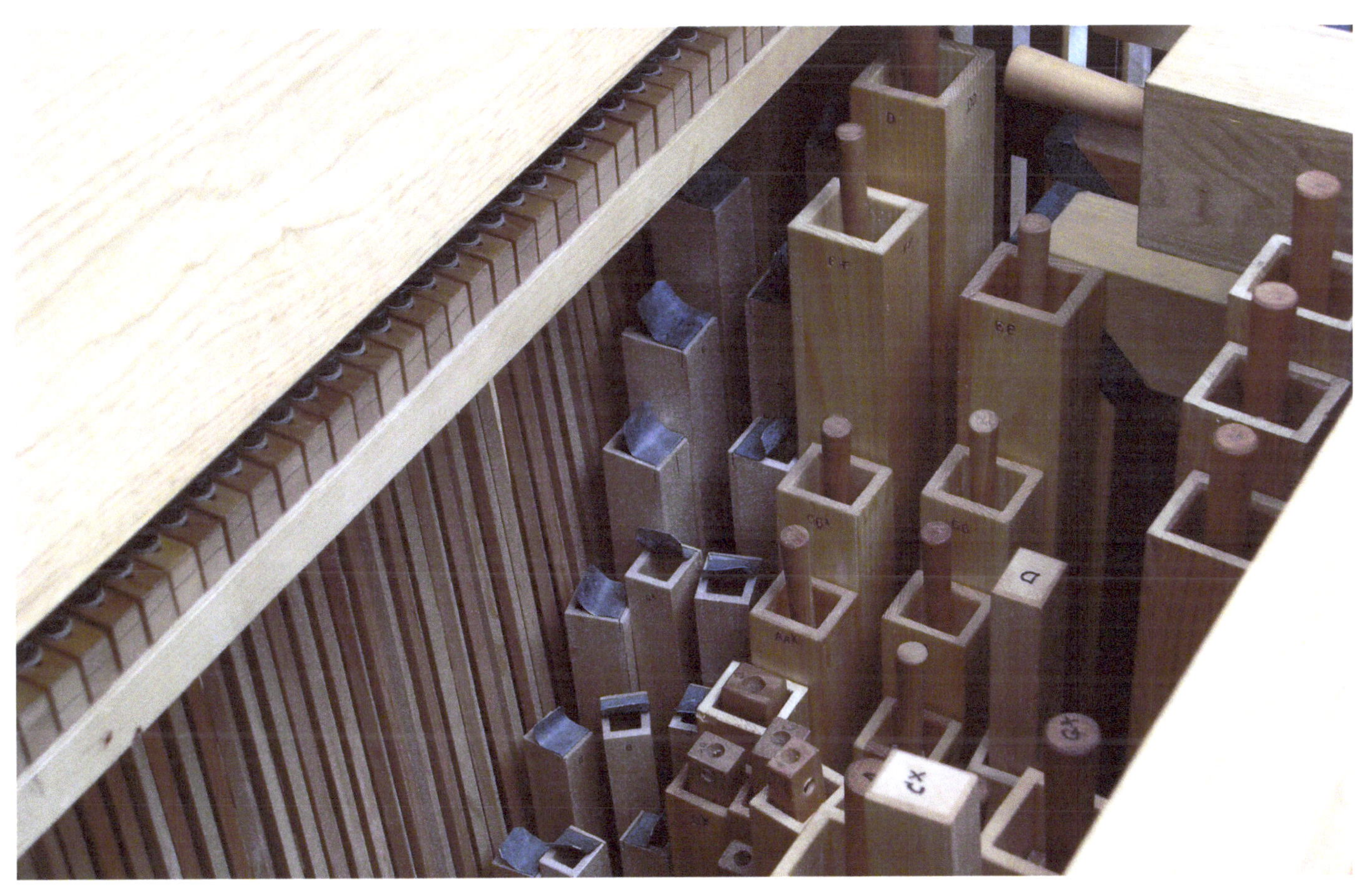

Pedal Pipes

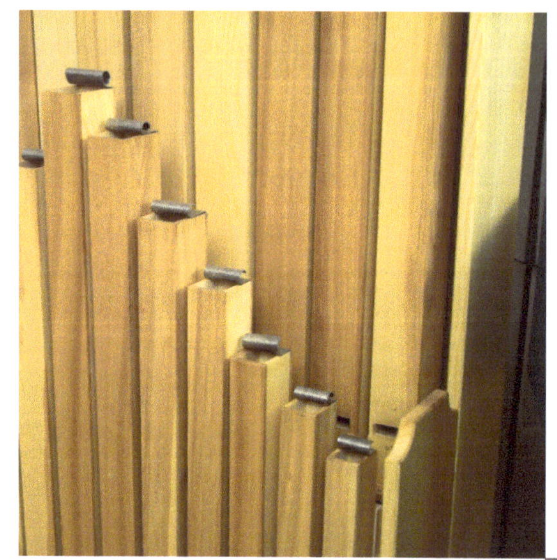

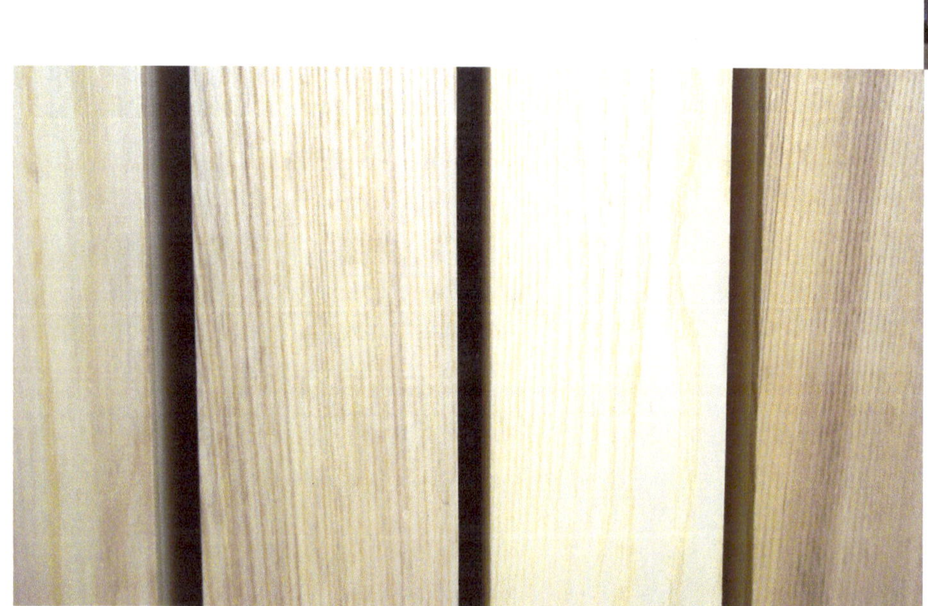

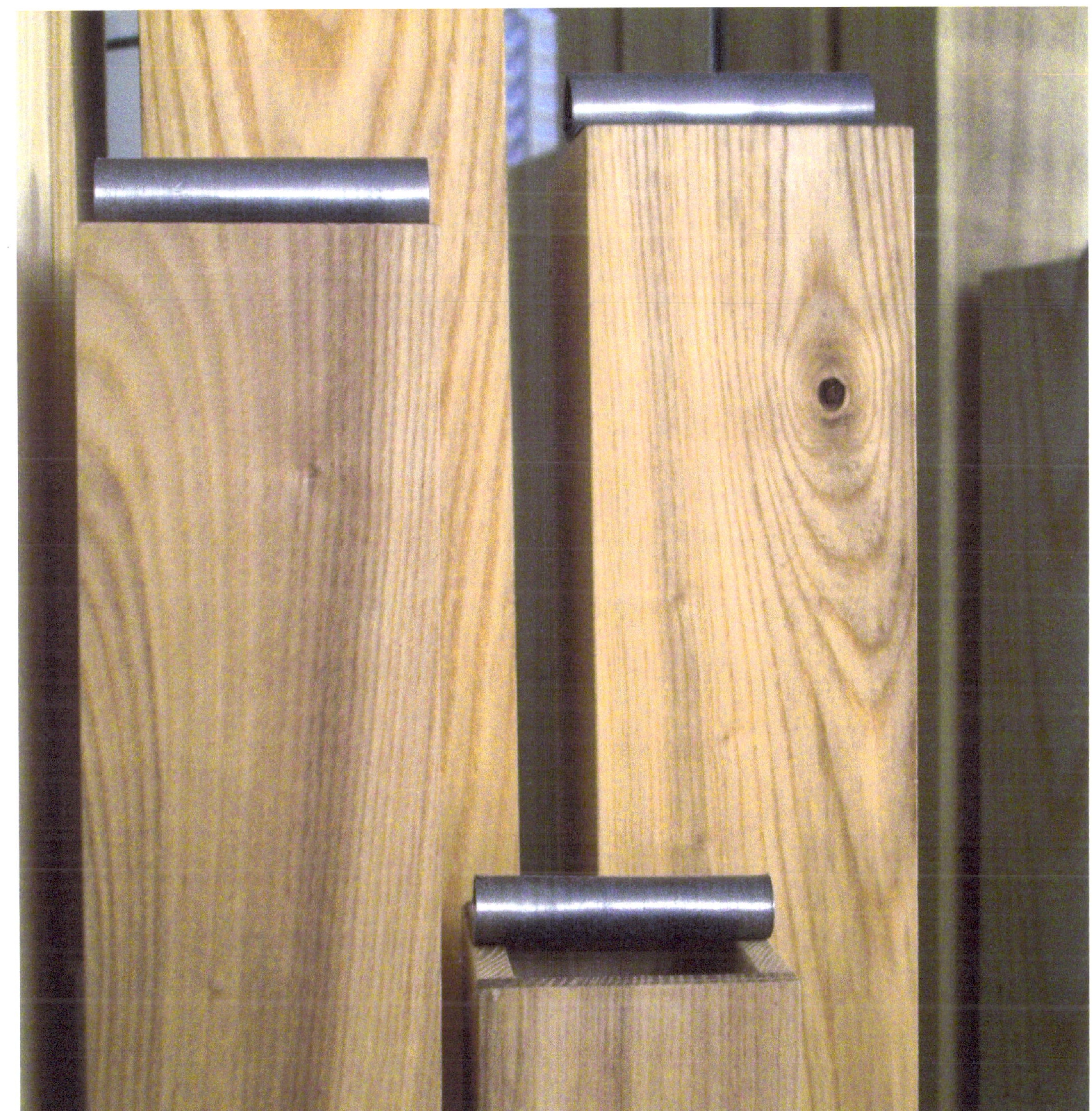

Keyboard, Pedalboard, and Case Details

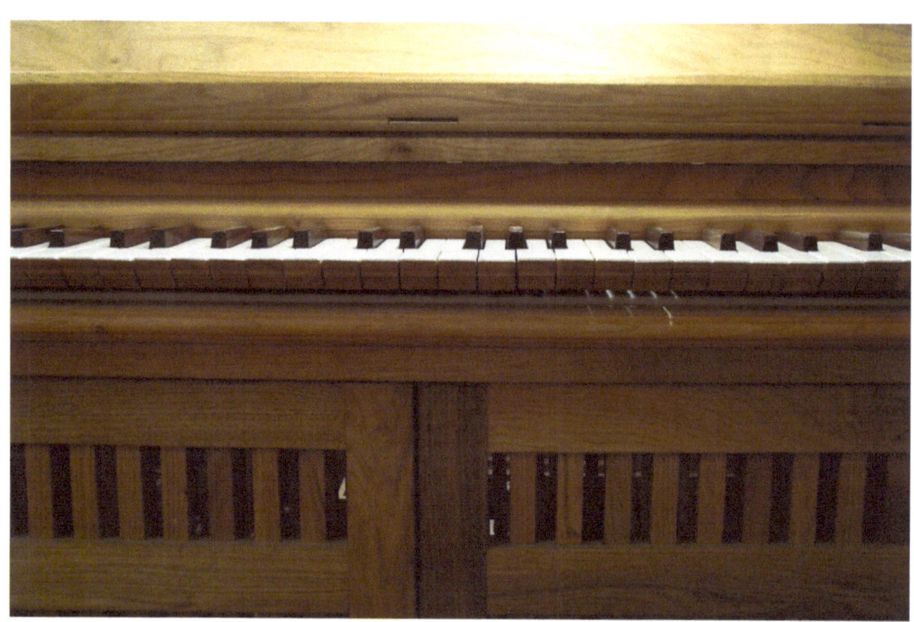

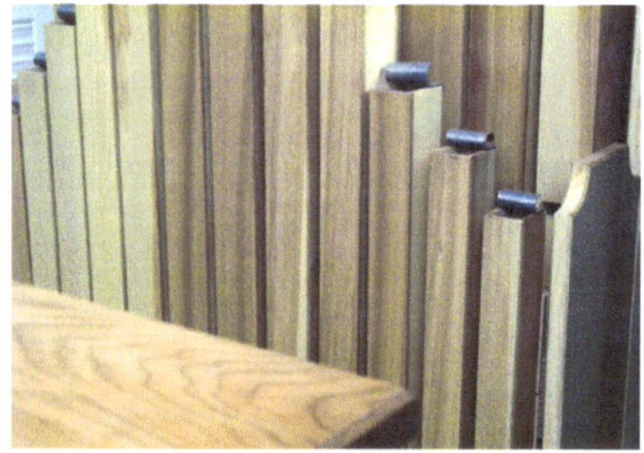

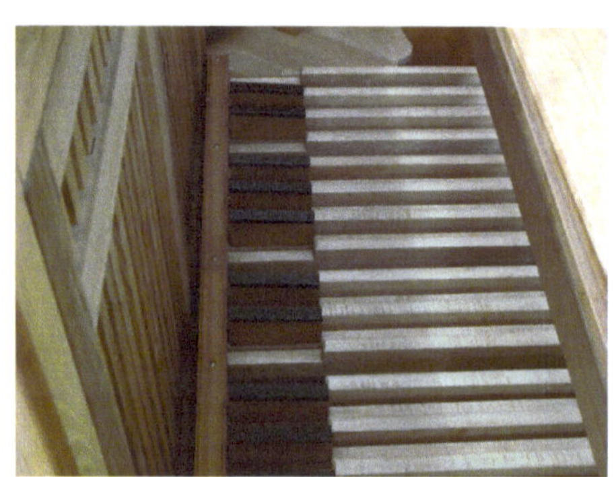

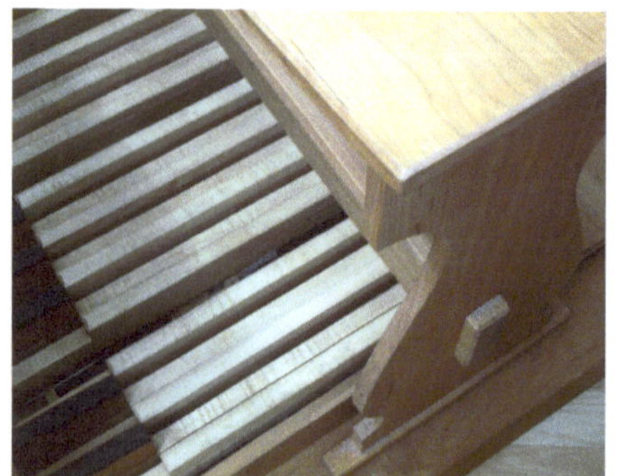

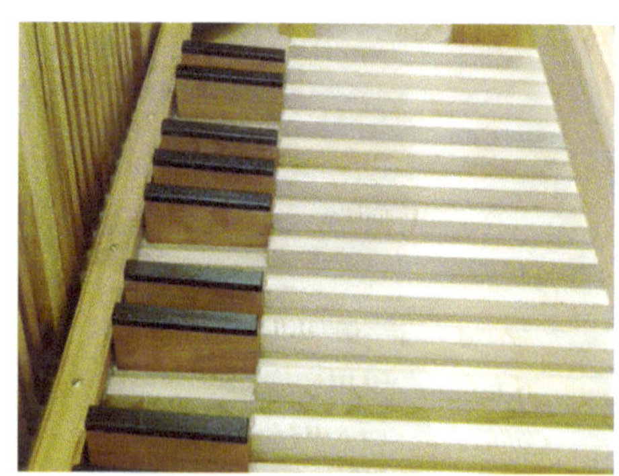

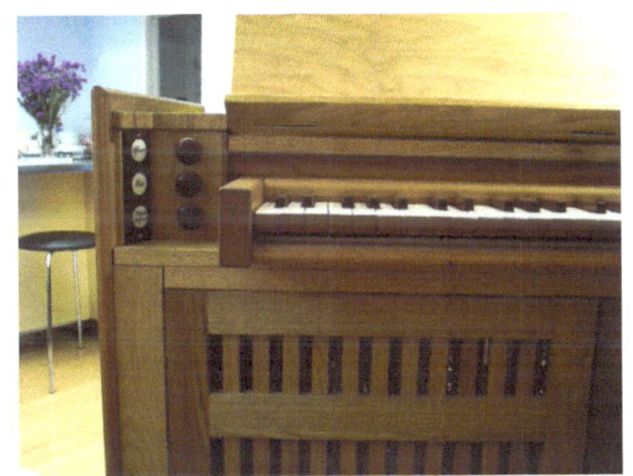

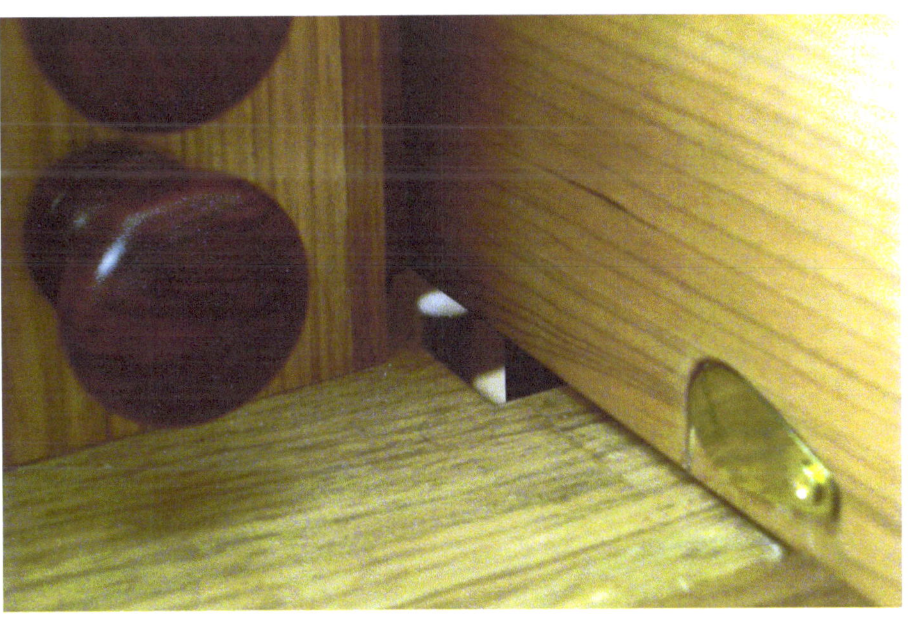

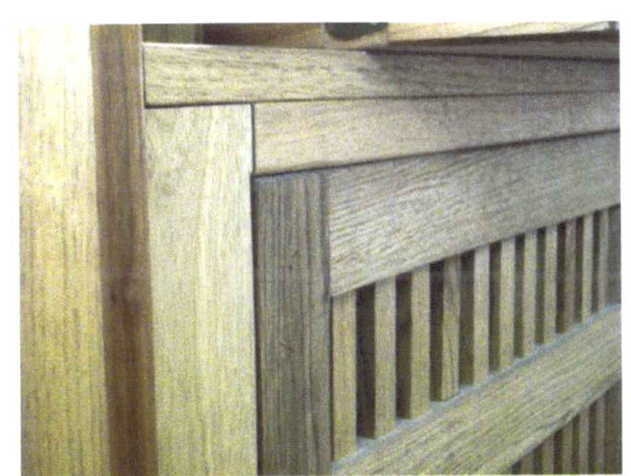

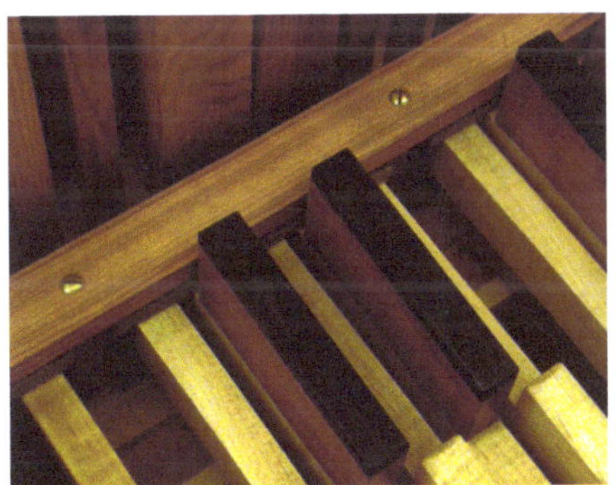

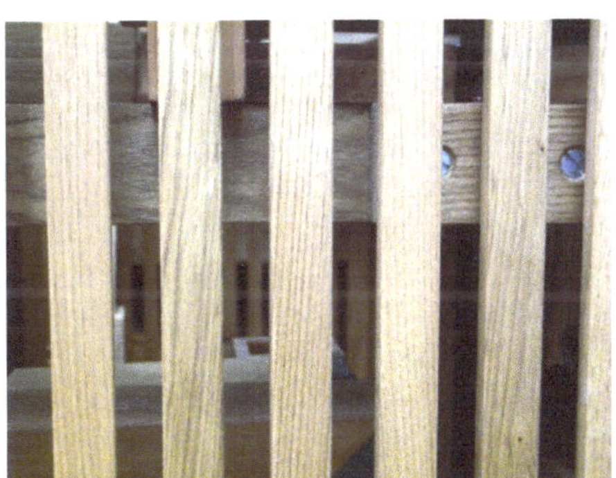

Interior Views

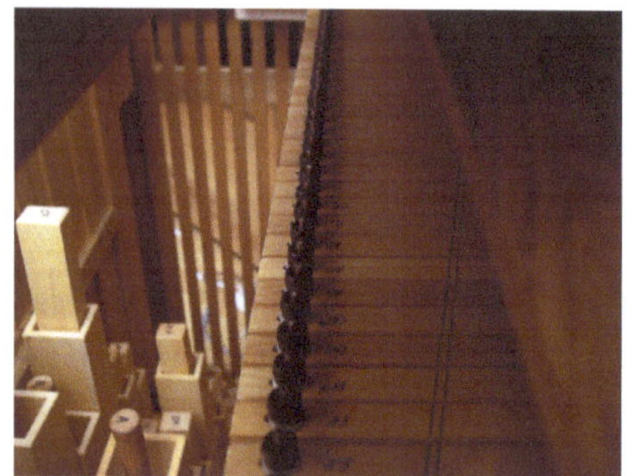

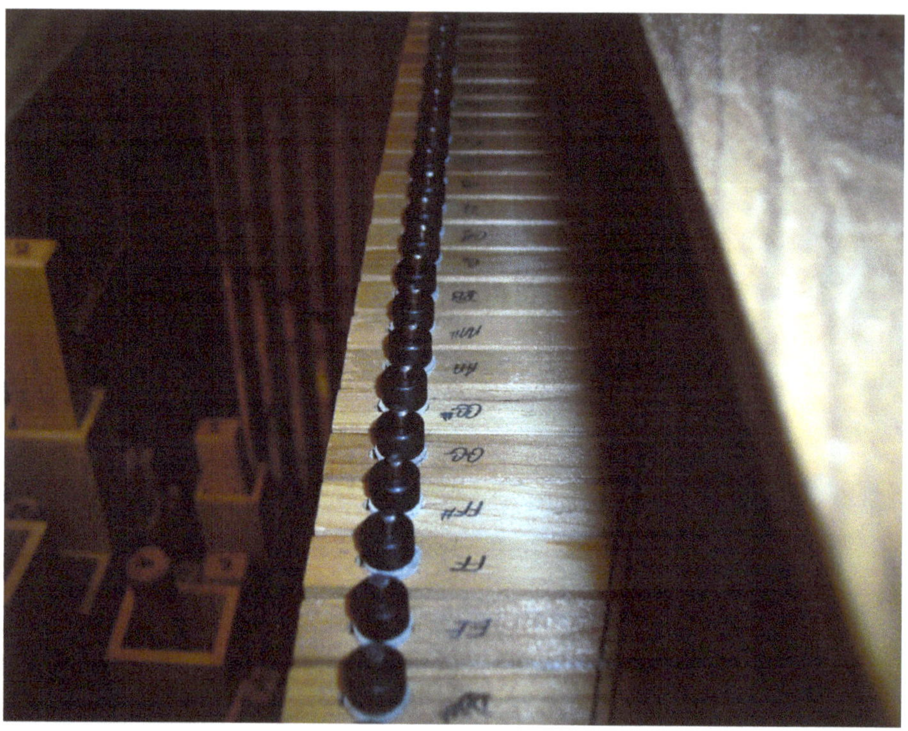

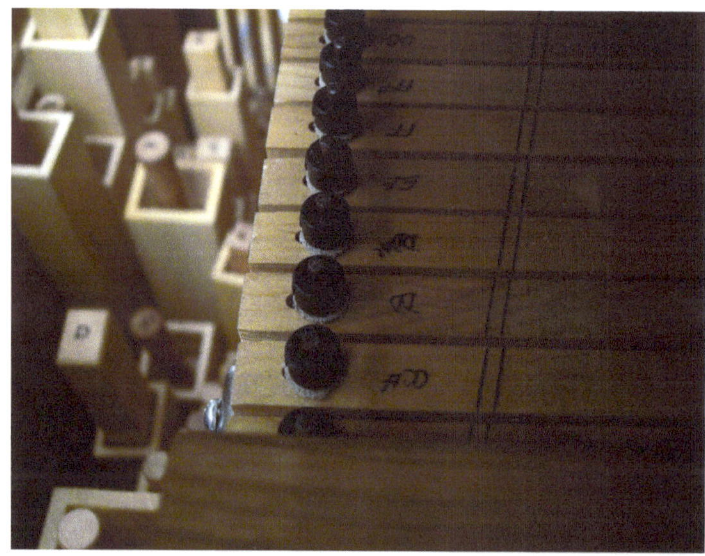

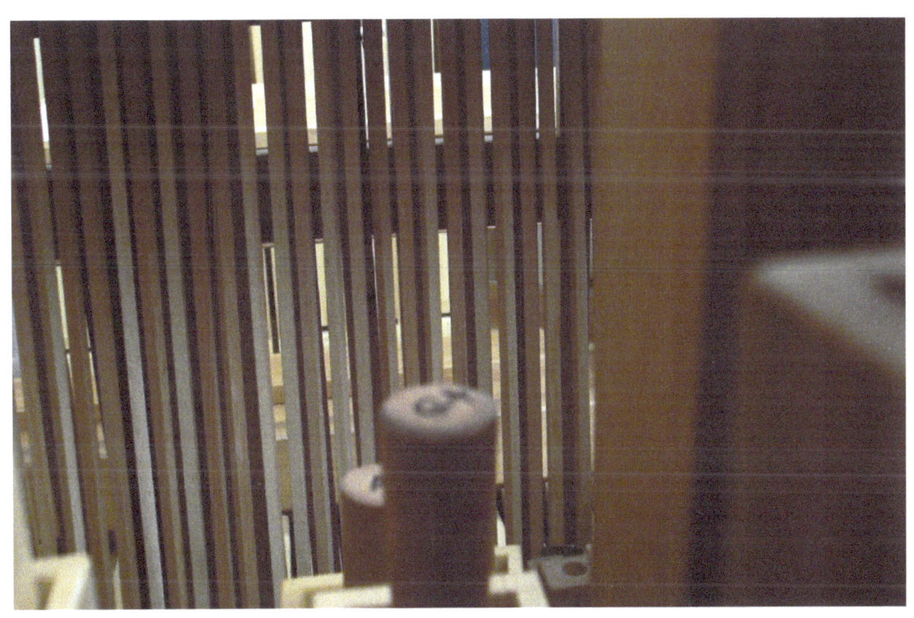

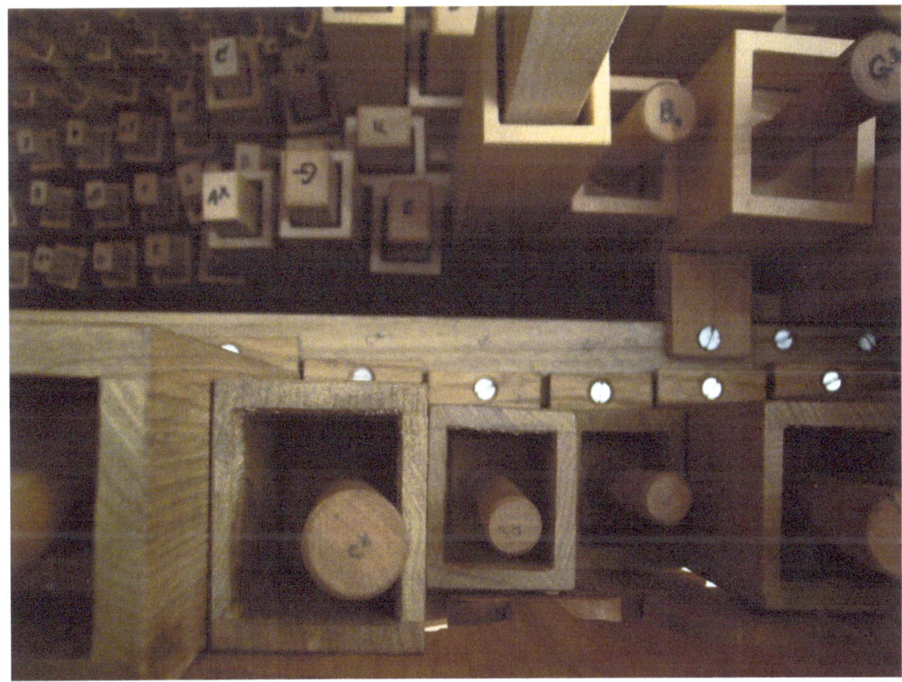

Video Stills

A. David Moore plays Opus 28 Emily

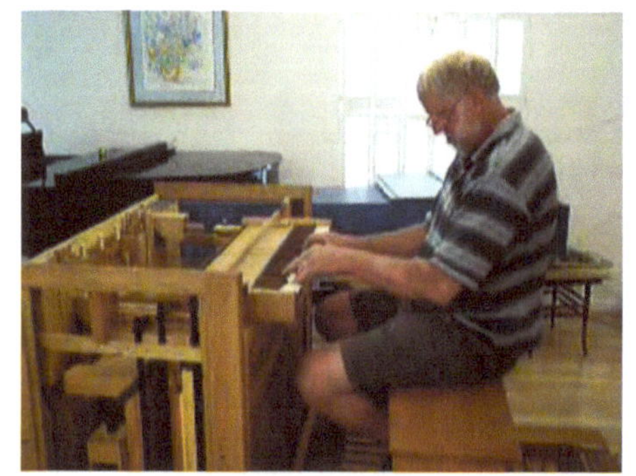
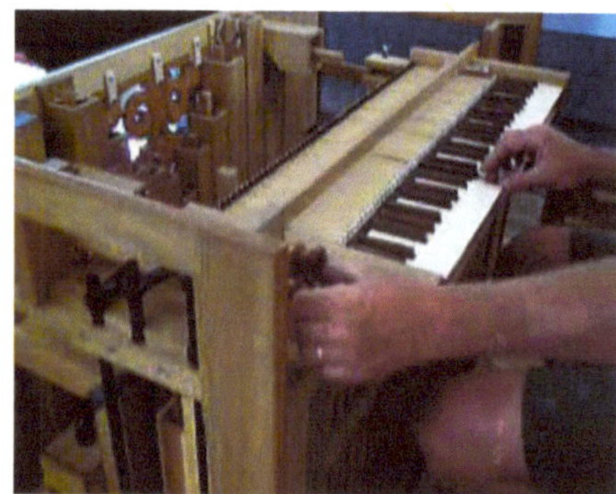
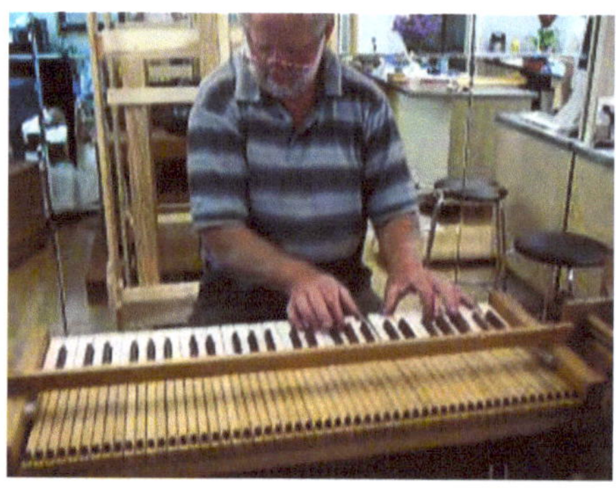
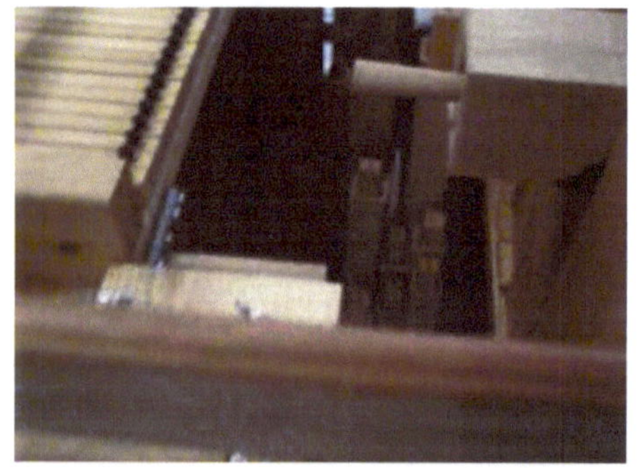
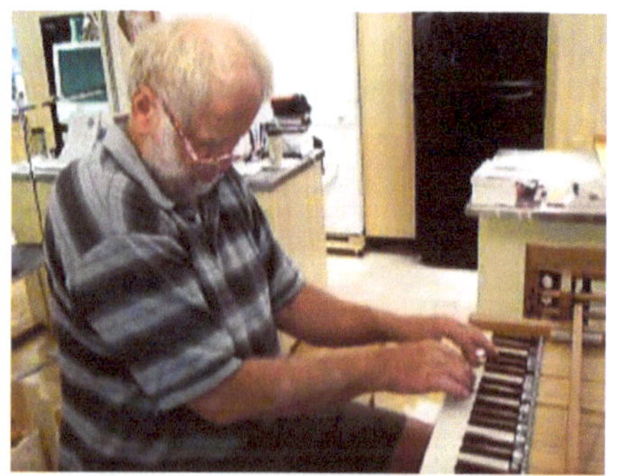
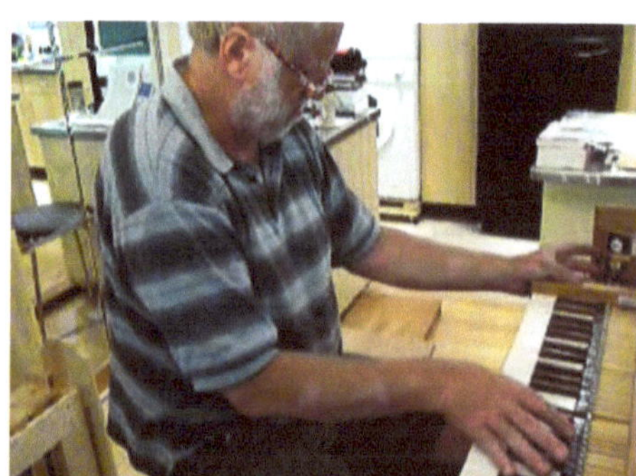
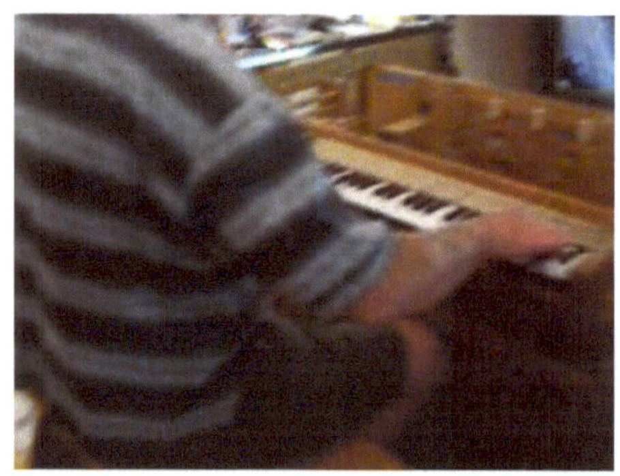
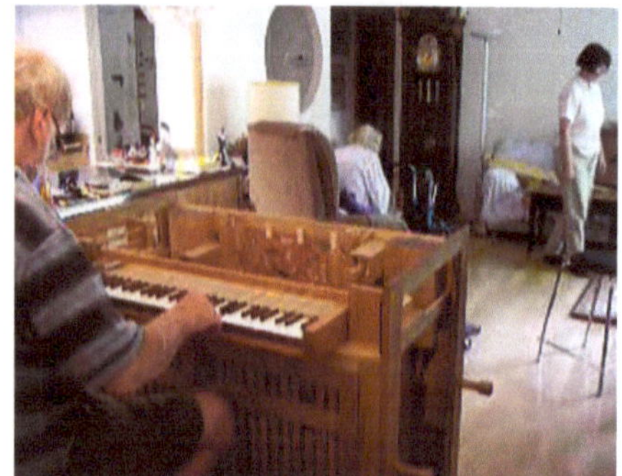
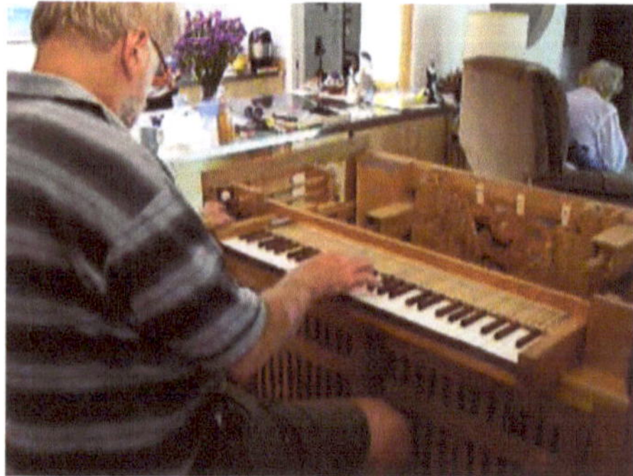

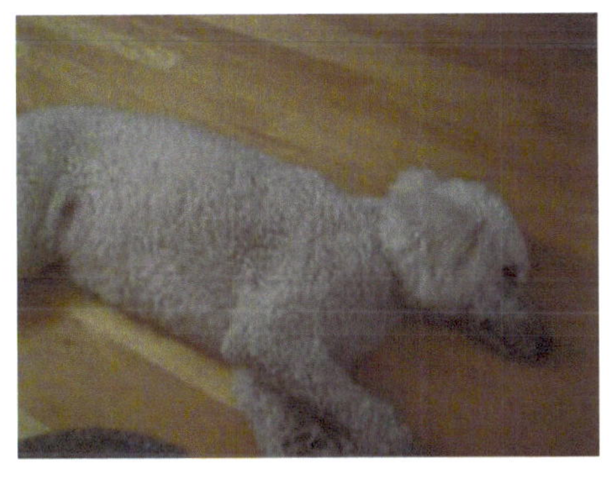
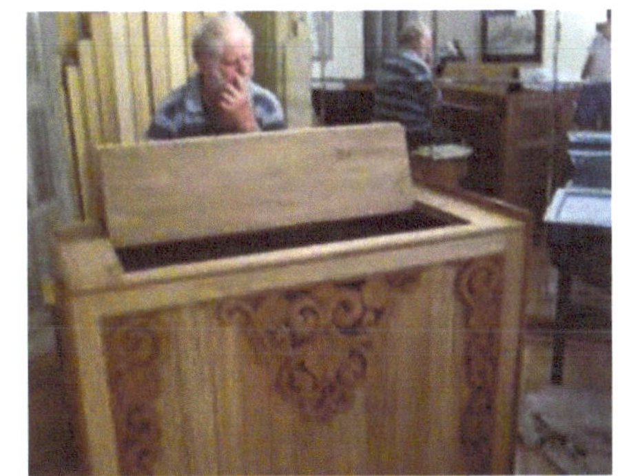
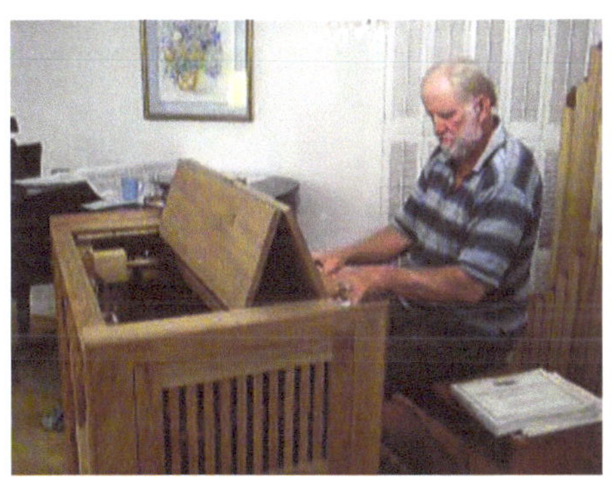

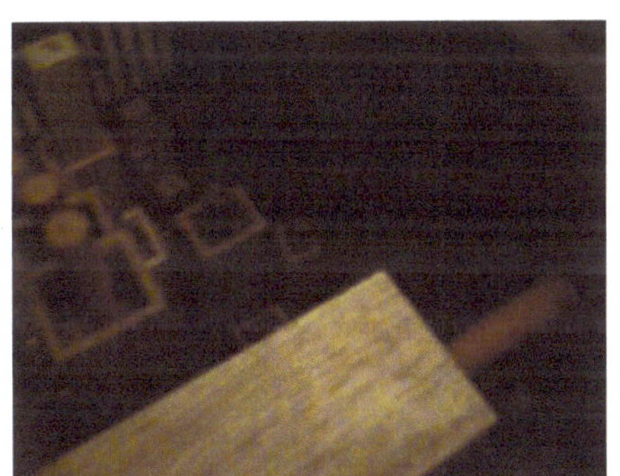
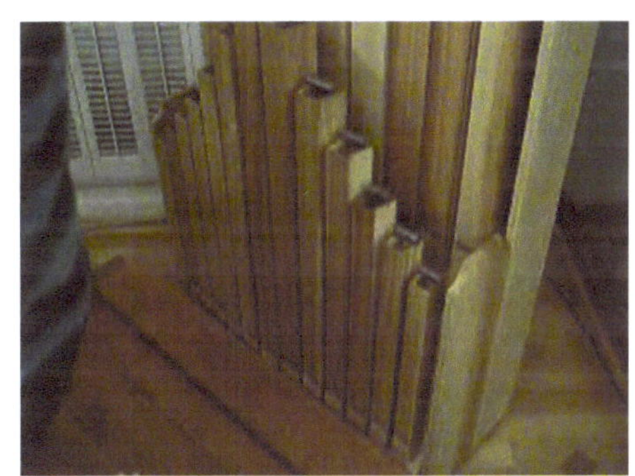
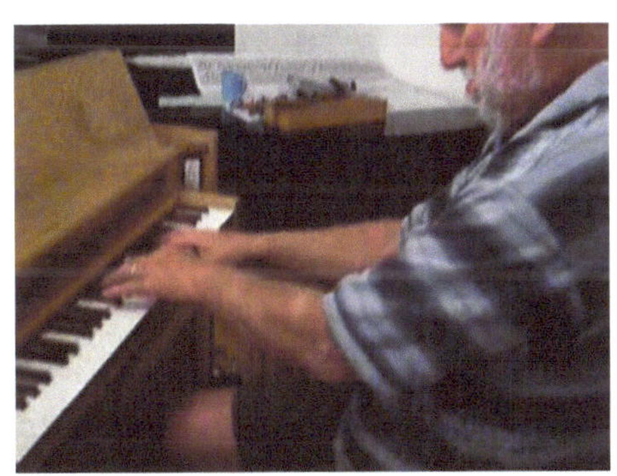
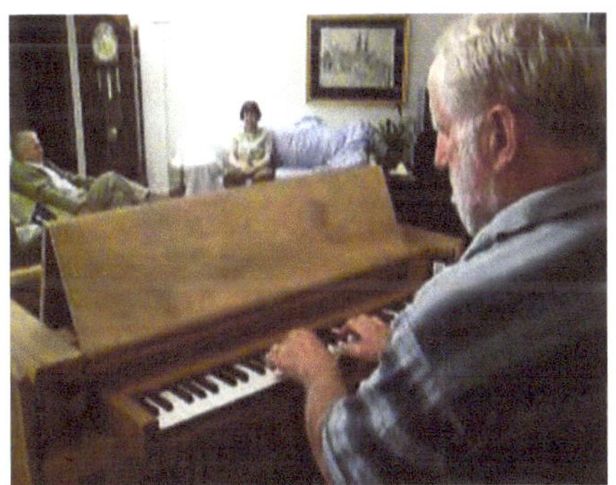
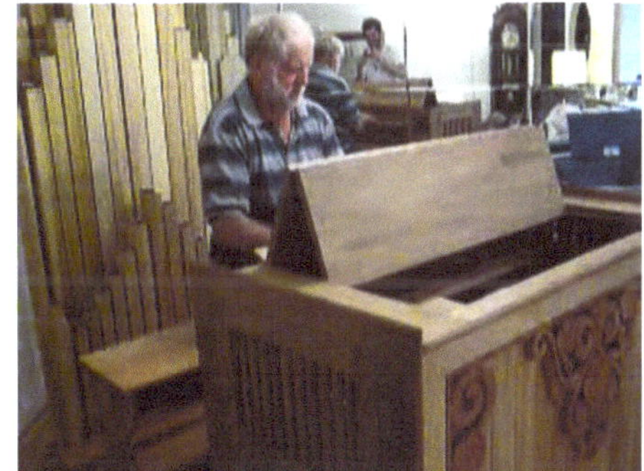

Miriam Zach plays Opus 28 Emily

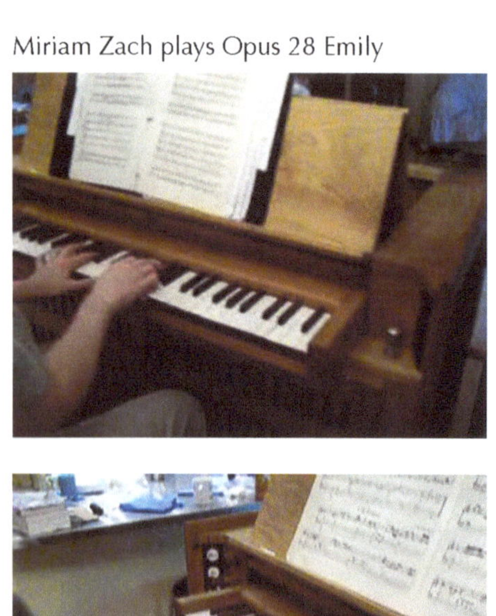

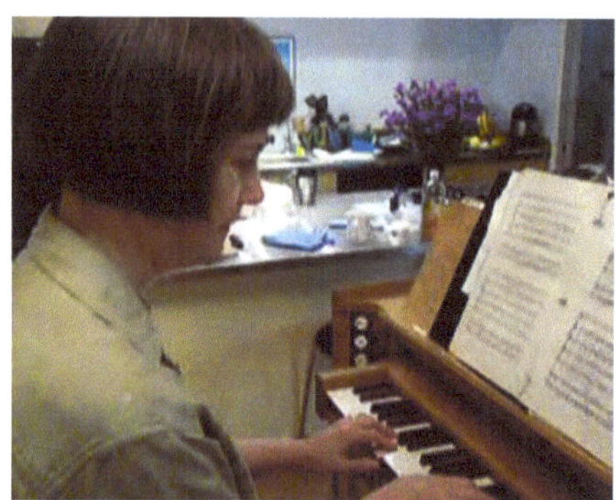

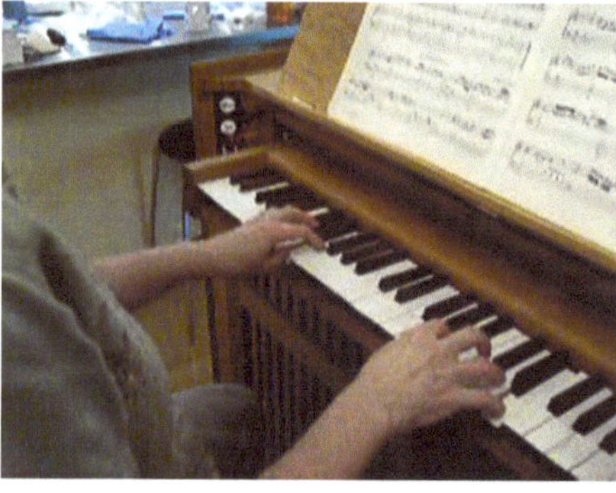

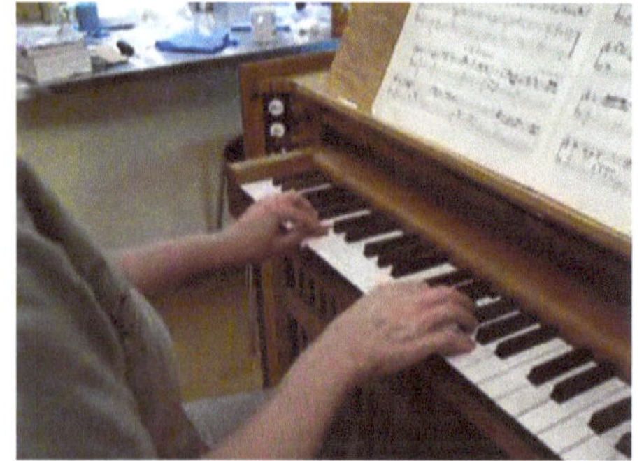

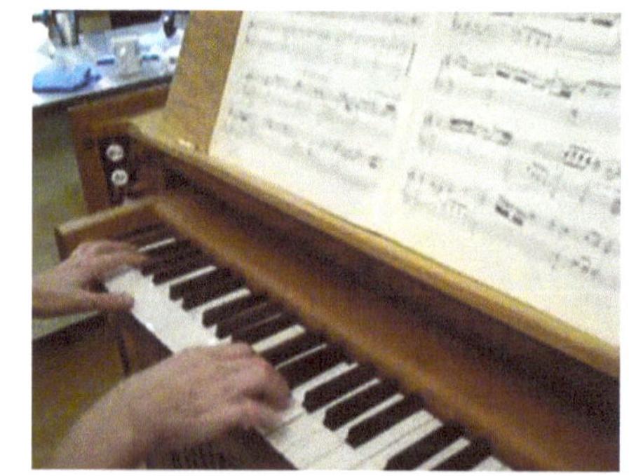

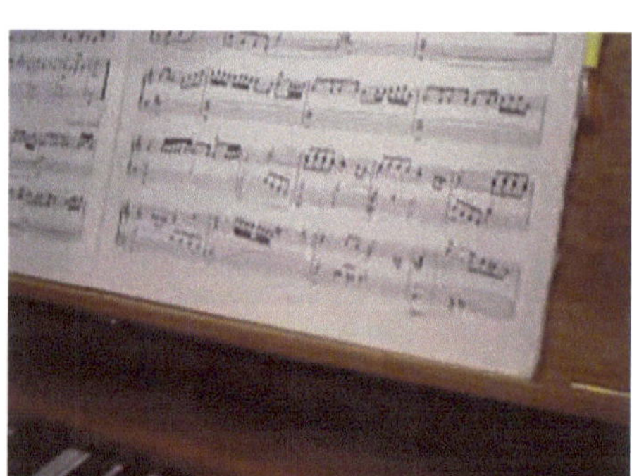

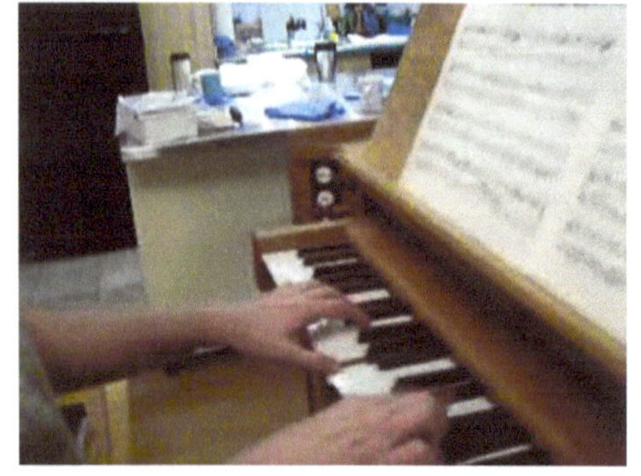

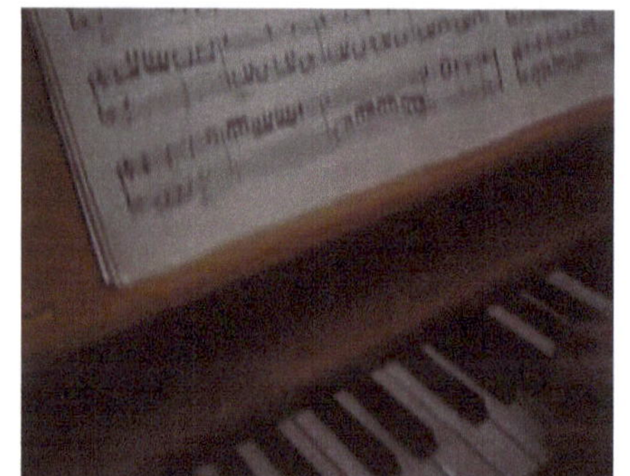

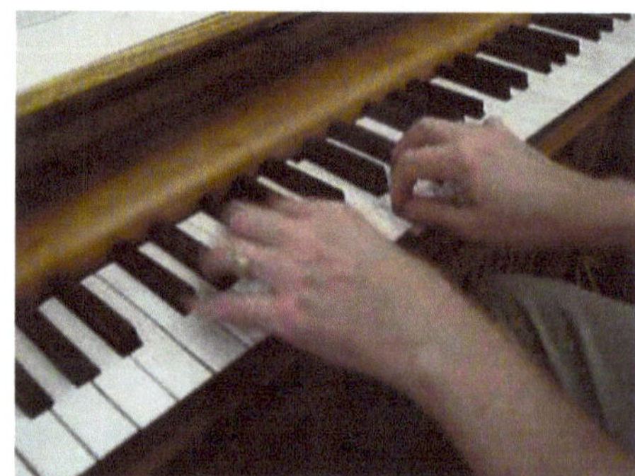

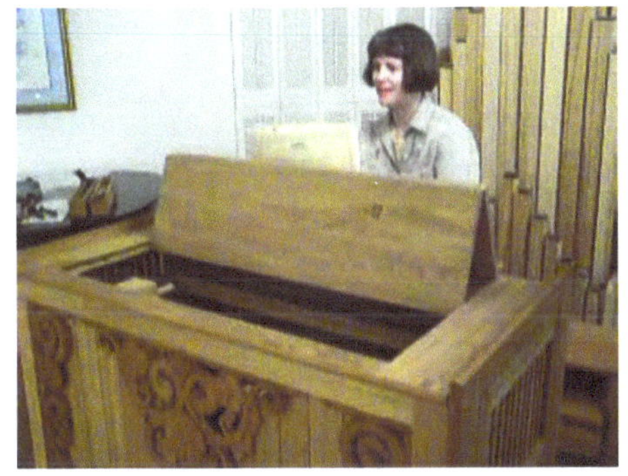
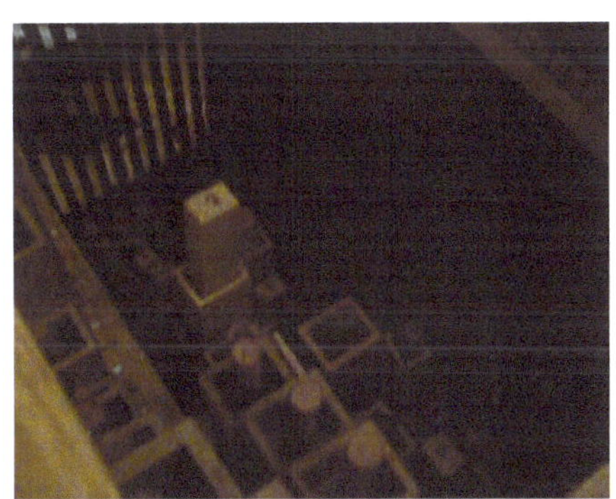
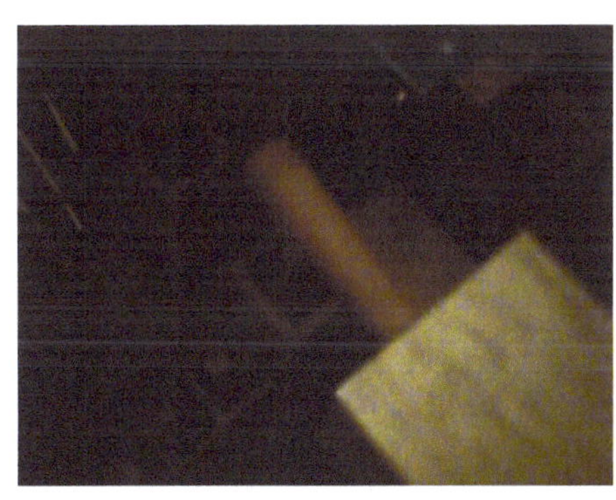
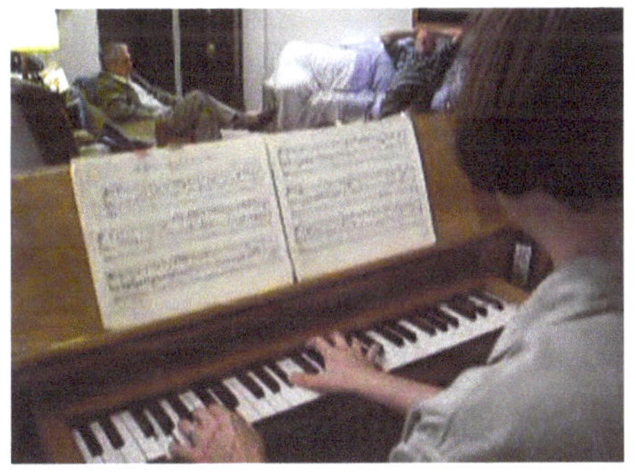
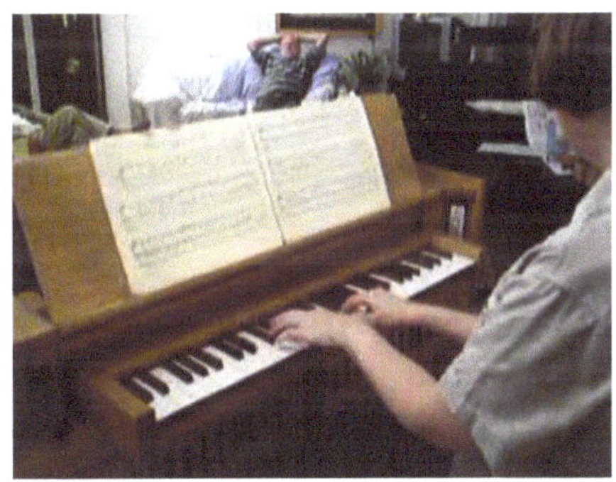
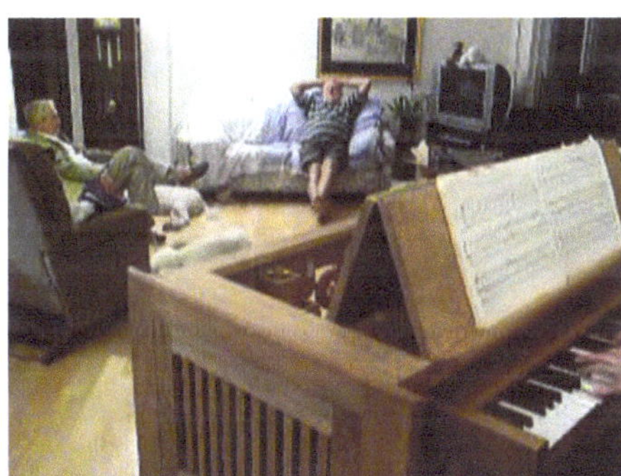

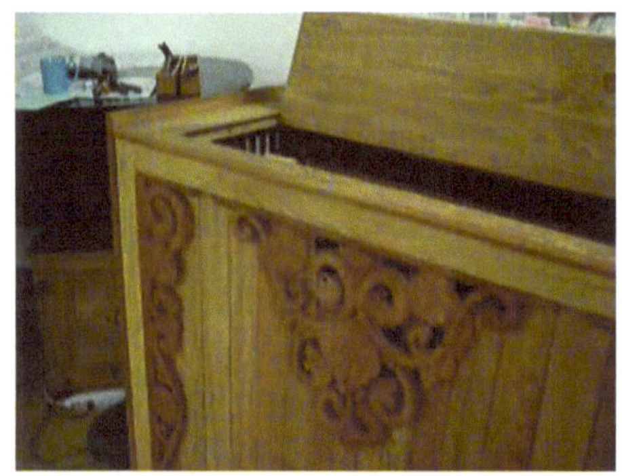

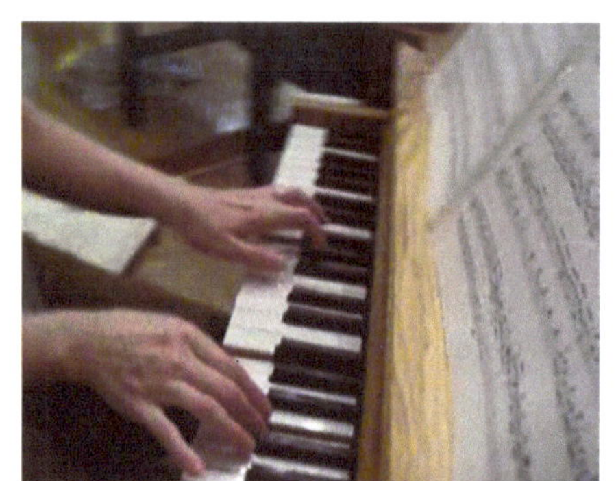

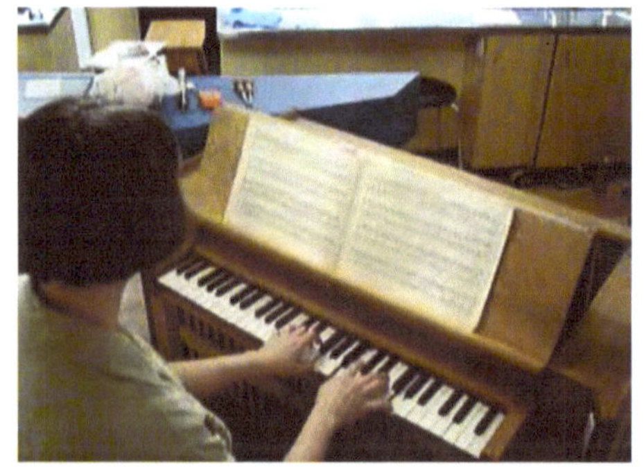

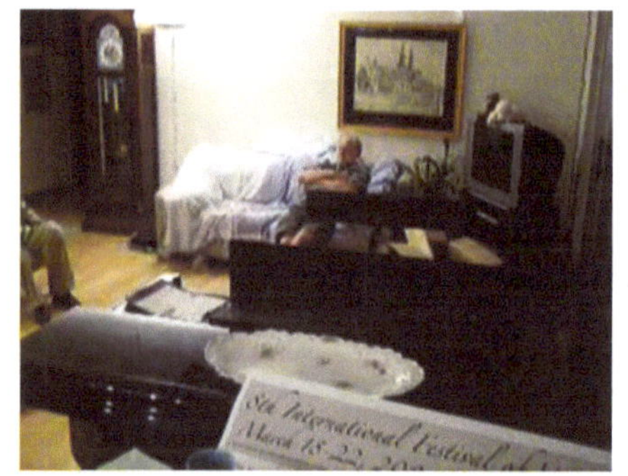

8th International Festival

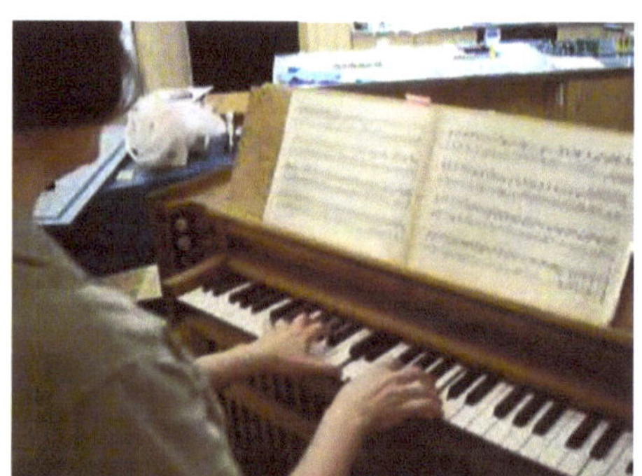

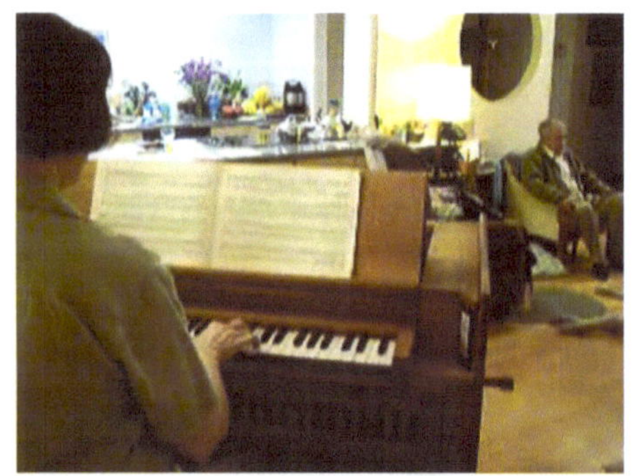

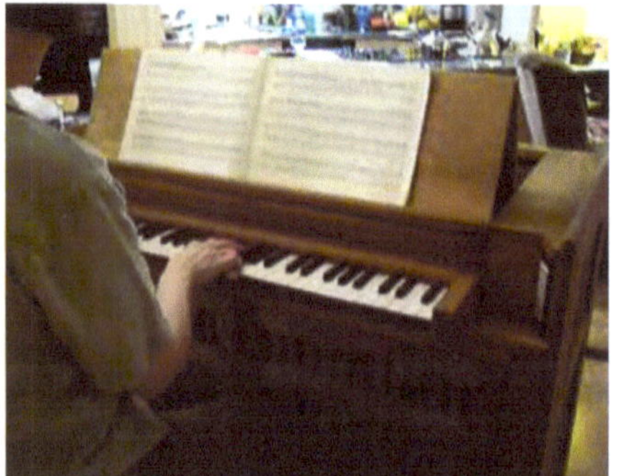

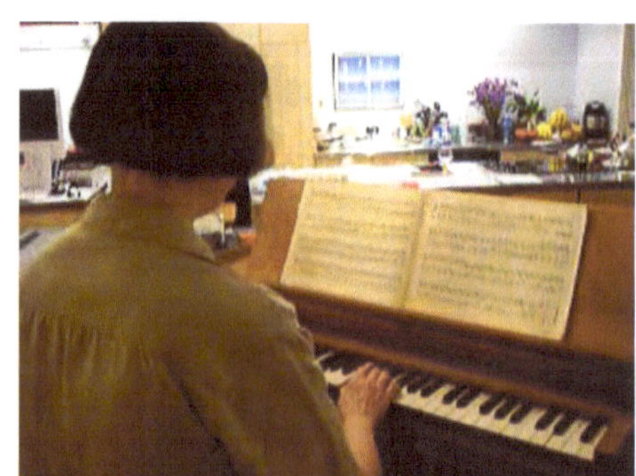

About A. David Moore

This story about A. David Moore was taken from the following website:http://www.georgan.com/moore.html, accessed Friday, May 19, 2006, at 5:03pm in Nina Mücke's apartment in Berlin, Germany.

David Moore is a North Pomfret Vermont native whose fomal schooling was completely in Vermont. He holds a degree from the University of Vermont. He lives and has his workshop on the large rural farm where he grew up.

(...)

I first met Dave Moore in 1970 when he was renting an apartment in the Pigeon Cove house of Charlie and Ann Fisk. David apprenticed in the then small Fisk shop before establishing his own workshop in North Pomfret, Vermont where he has been designing and building historically informed mechanical action organs for over three decades. This unique builder has traveled extensively and studied some of the finest old (and some new) organs of Germany, France, the Netherlands, Denmark, Italy and England. He has a working knowledge of the treatises of Cliquot and Dom Bédos. Living and working in New England, he has acquired a knowledge, both intimate and scholarly, of the 18th and 19th century New England builders. His association with the likes of John Fesperman, Barbara Owen, Fenner Douglass, Mark Brombaugh and Kevin Birch (to name but a few) has contributed to his understanding of the organ and its music.

(...)

Dr. Kevin Birch, music director of St. John's R.C. Church in Bangor, Maine, writes in his scholarly essay "A. David Moore, Organ Builder: An Account of His Work (1971-1994)" as follows:

"In the twenty-five years that he has been building organs, A. David Moore has earned a reputation as an important builder of his generation. Future players and builders will, no doubt, benefit from his work . . . the instruments by A. David Moore reflect the work of a gifted organ builder whose sound ideal continues to be influenced by his spirit of inquiry and by his appreciation of the enduring beauty of the old organs which inspire us all."

To hear samples of Emily's voice please direct your browser to

http://www.iwclib.org

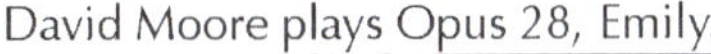
David Moore plays Opus 28, Emily.

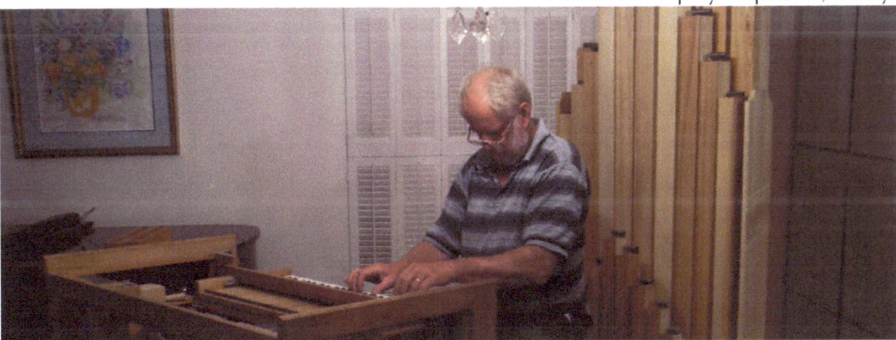

About the International Women Composers Library

In the history of music, the availability of scores, recordings, and books affects the formation of repertorial canons that determine what is performed and heard in concert halls and worship services. This consequently shapes cultural expectations of specific works and selects composers to be included in the educational process of future musicians. Until now music composed by women has been marginal to the standard repertoire of performers. This does not indicate a lack of the existence of women composers, but rather a lack of societal awareness and encouragement on their behalf.

I. The International Women Composers Library in Gainesville, Florida, was founded in the fall of 1994 in order to build a non-circulating research collection of manuscripts, published scores and books, commercial and private recordings, correspondence, interviews, theses, dissertations and other documents by and about women composers. The Library is directed by and based on the holdings assembled by Dr. Miriam S. Zach. The collection functions as a high profile entity for the advancement of women's creative efforts in music. It builds on the work of Antje Olivier, former Director of the Internationale Komponistinnen Bibliothek, Nicolaistrasse 2, 59423 Unna/Westfalen, Germany, already home of more than 9000 compositions and recordings by women. Although the North American Library operates as a non-for-profit organization, patrons are asked to pay a membership fee to gain access to the library.

II. The library functions as a resource to draw musicologists, performers, and music educators to conferences, workshops, and courses. Local community musical organizations have ready access to the collection to expand their performance repertoires. The Library operates not only as a depository of women's achievements over five millennia but also as a place of action/interaction, i.e. a cultural crossroads for those involved in advancing the status of women in music and related fields. The goal of the library is to expand the involvement of women in music composition in order to empower them to actively participate in the long history of women's productions in music. Although recent international and national symposia, music textbooks, articles in professional journals and recordings indicate a growing dissemination and acceptance of the important contributions of women to the arts, many non-music professionals are unaware of this information.

III. In addition to the establishment of the International Women Composers Library as an institution, one of its strengths is the engendering of international collaborative work and scientific meetings to share research findings, fostered by internet resources. To facilitate this exchange the Library is actively engaged to secure funding for the following research activities:

— the preparation of reference materials such as a catalogue of holdings, indices, electronic databases including internet access via a projected world-wide-web server on women's music.

— planning and implementation of humanities projects in other libraries and archives.

— periodic scholarly publications to prepare authoritative and annotated editions of works and documents through the IWCL's publication arm Culicidae Press.

For requests, donations, and comments please contact

miriamzach@gmail.com

To hear samples of Emily's voice please direct your browser to

http://www.iwclib.org

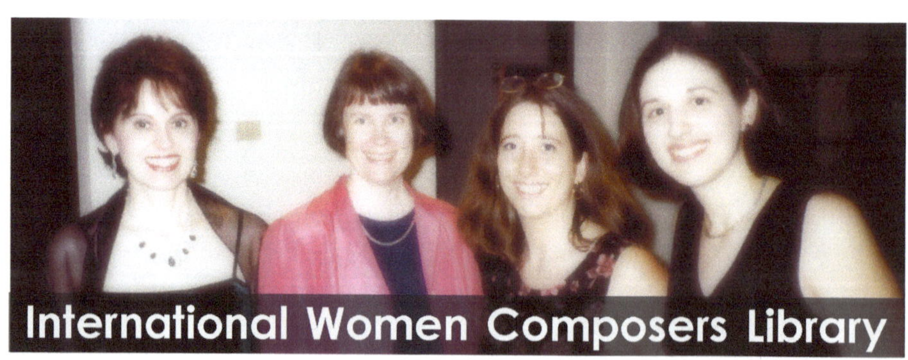

www.ingramcontent.com/pod-product-compliance
Lightning Source LLC
LaVergne TN
LVHW070149110826
845147LV00002B/359

9781941892206